HAMLYN ALL COLOUR
GREENHOUSE GARDENING

HAMLYN ALL COLOUR
GREENHOUSE GARDENING

HAMLYN

Art Editor Susan Michniewicz Editor Selina Higgins
Picture Research Liz Fowler Production Nick Thompson

Illustrations by Vicky Emptage
Symbols by Coryn Dickman

First published in Great Britain in 1993
by Hamlyn an imprint of Reed Consumer Books Limited
Michelin House, 81 Fulham Road, London SW3 6RB
and Auckland, Melbourne, Singapore and Toronto

A catalogue record for this book is available
from the British Library

ISBN 0 600 57644 2

Typeset in Sabon

Produced by Mandarin Offset
Printed in Hong Kong

The Publishers would like to thank the following organizations and individuals
for their kind permission to reproduce the photographs in this book.

A-Z Botanical Collection 26 left; 32 left; 46 right; 57 right; 75 right; 126 right; Boys Syndication/Jacqui Hurst 13,
94 right /Michael Boys title page centre, 19, 69 right, 76 left, 99 right, 107 right, 112, 116 right, 120;
Eric Crichton Photos, front cover right, title page left, 14, 20 left/back cover bottom left, 22 left, 24 right,
25 right, 27, 29 right, 30, 31 left, 32 right, 33 right, 38 right, 39 right, 40 left, 41 left, 42, 43 left, 44 right,
45, 47, 48 left, 51, 55/back cover top left, 56 right, 57 left, 58, 60 left, 61 left, 63 left, 64 left, 65 left,
67 left, 68/front cover left, 69 left, 70 right, 71 right, 73, 74, 76 right, 78, 82 left, 83 left, 85, 86 right,
95, 96 right, 99 left, 102 right, 103 right, 110 left, 118 left, 119 right, 121, 123 left, 124 left;
John Glover 91, 108 right; Jerry Harpur 28 left, 97 right, 98 left;
Neil Holmes 24 left, 34 left, 37, 38 left, 44 right, 46 left, 52 right, 62 left, 64 right,
72 left, 79 right, 96 left, 107 left, 108 left, 116 left, 117 left, 118 right;
Hulton-Deutsch Collection 12, 15; Tania Midgely 98 right; John Moss 75 left; Clive Nichols 81;
Photos Horticultural 6, 25 left, 49 right, 50 right, 52 left, 65 right, 67 right, 82 right, 83 right, 95 left,
113, 115 left, 119 left; Reed International Books Ltd, 124 right, /Michael Boys, back cover centre, 44 left,
56 left, 70 left, 71 left, 79 left, 104, /M. Crockett 9, /Jerry Harpur half title, title page right, 18,
20 right, 22 right, 29 left, 92 left/back cover top right, 92 right, 94 left, 98 left, 101, 102 left,
/W.F. Davidson 31 right, 33 left, 35 right/front cover centre, 39 left, 40 right, 41 right, 56 left,
59 right, 77 right, 93 left, /Neil Holmes 48 right, 87 right, 88 left, 97 left, 110 right, 117 right,
/George Wright 54, 62 right, 72 right, 115 right; Harry Smith Collection 21, 88 right, 105, 106 right,
109 right, 111, 114 left; Peter Stiles 23, 26 right, 35 left, 36, 49 left, 50 left, 53 left, 60 right,
61 right, 63 right, 66, 77 left, 80 top & bottom, 84, 86 left, 89, 90; 106 left, 109 left, 114 right,
122, 123 right, 125 left; Judy Todd, back cover bottom right, 34 right, 59 left, 87 left;
George Wright 28 right, 53 right, 93 right, 100, 103 left

CONTENTS

IN THE GREENHOUSE

Greenhouses give gardening that crucial, extra dimension. They are the equivalent of the scientist's laboratory. Here you coax tiny gardenia cuttings into 1.2m/4ft high scented shrubs, pick kiwi fruit, figs and grapes, eat fresh strawberries months before they ripen outside, and start a collection of jaw-trapping insect-swallowing plants.

Cold greenhouses certainly limit your choices, though if you can provide portable heat and maintain a minimum winter temperature of 5°C/40°F you can grow as good a range of plants as anyone, anywhere could hope for. They include the chocolate-scented *Cosmos atrosanguineus* and the bustling blue daisies of *Felicia amelloides* 'Santa Anita'. Increase the heat and you end up with high-performance tropical exotica.

Of course things never go entirely to plan. Chaos takes over. Rooting powder flits up the nose, a pot of basil expands to eight trial varieties featuring Thai and Mexican which take up the whole bench, whitefly whirl in and out, abutilon's plum-coloured bells get tangled in the pineapple guava, and fungal disease regularly threatens to wipe out the lot. But no matter. Life with a greenhouse is invariably richer than life without one. As the following plant entries make clear, the plant world comes just that little bit more alive.

GREENHOUSE SELECTION

When you've decided how much space you can allot to a greenhouse, and the range of plants to be grown, examine the different types for design, material, covering, size, and heating.

DESIGN This means either lean-to or free-standing. The former has the benefit of extra, natural heat when a glass side is replaced by a heat-retaining wall. Furthermore if the lean-to encloses the back door of the house it traps escaping heat and invariably guarantees a frost-free winter. The disadvantage is that even when built against a warm, sunny wall the lean-to is in the shade for at least part of the day. This is not ideal for growing tomatoes, or propagation.

Provided the free-standing greenhouse is sensibly sited it automatically receives more light. Manufacturers have recently become more inventive and now provide circular versions in addition to the traditional rectangular shape. Some have attractive domed roofs and make fine, albeit expensive, garden features.

The lean-to and free-standing greenhouse can be either glass from ground to roof, or have a waist-high lower section. The former lets in more light (vital for growing vegetables in the border), the latter provides extra insulation and is the better option for growing flowering plants. Pots can be stood on the bench, with bulbs, bags of soil, etc., stored beneath during winter.

MATERIAL Aluminium greenhouses are cheaper to buy but can be quite an eye-sore, whereas the red/brown cedar wood could not look better. It's mainly a question of cost, though the aluminium bars do tend to be slightly narrower than wooden ones and let in more light. Wood, on the other hand, is marginally more efficient at retaining heat. It's also much easier for putting up shelves where you want them; you don't have to drill holes in the metal. Just occasionally though the wood does need treating with wood preservative to retain colour and prevent rotting.

COVERING The main alternative is plastic, as in the mobile polythene tunnel. You can site it over one part of the vegetable garden in early spring and treat it as a giant cloche; then use elsewhere, all summer long, for tomatoes etc.; and finally stand over a late-season fruiting crop. The main problem is the more it's

7

moved, the greater the likelihood of torn plastic. It is generally reckoned that the covering won't last more than three or four years before running repairs, or a complete replacement, is required.

If your conventional greenhouse is packed to the limit then the polythene tunnel is an excellent way of creating extra inexpensive room.

SIZE Quite simply, the bigger the better. Not only do small greenhouses overheat in mid-summer, but they nearly always limit your ambitions. And once you've got a greenhouse those ambitions multiply. Two tomato plants, five seed trays, and a handful of tender, ornamental plants might initially seem fine, but when you see the results and start wanting to compare five different tomato varieties and grow ever more exotic plants then you'll certainly regret your decision. You shouldn't need anything larger than 2.7 x 3.3m/9 x 11ft size, though in most cases 1.8 x 2.4m/6 x 8ft is adequate. In any event ensure you buy the kind of greenhouse on which you can build extensions.

HEATING

Most people start with an unheated greenhouse, and add the heating later. Although it's generally assumed the cold greenhouse will be limiting, it's surprising how useful it can be. You can grow many of the same crops and ornamental plants as in a heated greenhouse, only you can't start so early in the year. You must wait for nature to provide the higher temperatures. You can also grow frost-tender plants such as fuchsias, and tuberous begonias provided you keep them in the greenhouse only from late spring to early autumn. Thereafter raise indoors on a windowsill.

The heated greenhouse extends the growing season, keeping tomatoes fruiting until near Christmas, which is out of the question in an unheated greenhouse in cold regions. It also enables you to bring 'tender perennials' into the warmth over winter. The term is partly relative and depends upon where you live. In mild, sheltered, protected gardens by the Gulf Stream you can probably leave an *Osteospermum* 'Buttermilk' outside all year round. But in an exposed chilly site the plant might die without winter protection.

PARAFFIN HEATERS They are more expensive to run than they used to be, but at least they are more sophisticated, with many models specifically manufactured for the greenhouse. They are essentially a plant 'life-saver', being used when the temperature gets close to freezing. However, there are two disadvantages. Firstly, you must have the time to light and turn them off. Secondly, you might decide to leave the heater running on a freezing morning but not be around later in the day to switch it off when the weather improves and the greenhouse temperature soars to high levels.

GAS HEATERS They are far more convenient, being available with thermostatic controls. Some run off the mains but they are usually more expensive than those needing gas cylinders. The advantage of both paraffin and gas is that you don't have to go to the expense of installing electricity.

ELECTRICITY This is the most reliable and economical form of heating. By using an accurate thermostat the heat is only on when you need it, and cuts out the moment the required temperature is reached. Also, electric heaters automatically switch themselves off and on. The one worry of course is a power cut, which is most likely in the severest winter weather. It pays to have a paraffin heater in reserve.

POSITION AND SITE

In a very small garden you won't have much choice where to site the greenhouse. It goes in the only available space. But if you do have a choice, you must apply certain important criteria.

LIGHT Place the greenhouse so that one end points to the rising sun, the other to the setting sun. Since the sun's path varies from summer to winter chose a line between the two extremes, guaranteeing maximum sunlight throughout the year.

This also means standing the greenhouse well away from shade cast by trees and buildings (not least to avoid damage from falling branches and dislodged roof slates), though some degree of shelter is necessary. Vulnerable sites can be improved by a wind-filtering hedge planted at a distance of three times the greenhouse height on the most exposed side. Nearby walls are not a good idea since they force the prevailing wind over and down, resulting in damaging turbulence.

SPADE WORK Preparing the foundation site involves making it level and uniformly firm. Many metal greenhouses now have pre-formed bases which are easily assembled. The base is set on top of the prepared soil with the greenhouse being bolted in place. If you don't buy the manufacturer's base, build a dwarf wall about three bricks high and assemble the greenhouse on top. Whether choosing brick or metal, it is essential the base is level from side to side, front to back, and across both diagonals. Always use a spirit level.

Before constructing the greenhouse lay out all the parts. Use a felt-tip pen to label each piece so you can see what it is and where it goes according to the plan. Assemble the structure flat on the ground, each side constructed in turn before being bolted to the base. The glazing bars in the roof are normally inserted last. Allow a complete day for assembling, and another day to glaze. Don't attempt the latter when you've only two more available hours because if left unfinished the structure can be damaged by the wind.

MAINTENANCE

Twice a year give the greenhouse a thorough clean. Once in the autumn, before tender plants are put under glass, and once in early spring before seed sowing begins. Having emptied the area scrub the frame, glass, staging, shelves, and floor if it's concrete, with hot water and detergent. Scrape off any moss or algae growing on the glass, and ensure no cracks appear between the sections of glass. Finally, rinse down with a strong jet from the hose pipe, and leave open the doors and ventilators to let the greenhouse dry. It's crucial to clean out any stacks of plant pots to eliminate pests and diseases, and to store them away on a shelf.

The second task involves preparing the borders for planting. Fork them over, and dig in plenty of peat, well-rotted manure or garden compost to improve the soil. Rake the soil level, and remove any large stones, dead leaves and other debris. There is no need to add

Paraffin heaters are a means of keeping the greenhouse frost-free in the winter months. Even though they have their disadvantages, any form of heating extends the growing season as outside temperatures drop.

fertilizer before planting or sowing in the autumn. However you should add a sprinkling of Growmore two weeks before a spring sowing.

BASIC EQUIPMENT

VENTILATORS Whenever the sun comes out the temperature inside the greenhouse rises sharply. But while plants like warmth, too much heat quickly dries them out and can be fatal. Ventilation keeps temperatures down to acceptable levels, enabling plants to thrive. Ideally you should keep the temperature below 27°C/81°F, though provided plants are well-watered they should be able to withstand slightly higher temperatures for brief periods.

Most greenhouses are equipped with a single ventilator in the roof. This is usually adequate, provided you are in constant attendance. If not, use an automatic appliance. They contain a special tube of paraffin wax which expands or contracts with a rise or fall in the temperature, extending or shortening a rod which in turn opens and closes the ventilator. Make certain that your model can support the required weight. The minimum is easily ascertained by resting the open window on a pair of household scales.

SHADING During mid-summer even good ventilation is inadequate at reducing the highest temperatures. Seedlings wilt and are sun-scorched. To overcome such problems shade the greenhouse. You can paint the outside with a special liquid, or attach protective 'bubble' sheeting within.

STAGING For maximum ventilation and humidity use corrugated iron sheets with holes drilled in to drain away water, and a short surrounding rim. Pour horticultural grit within, where the plant pots stand. The alternative is wooden slatted tables, which it must be said look much more attractive, and are far more easily purchased. However they're not much use for automatic watering systems. And plants dry out faster as the air whips through the gaps.

POTS They come in various sizes, such as 9cm/3½in, the figure denoting the distance across the top. Clay pots are useful for large, top-heavy plants, especially if they are going to stand outside over summer. Their weight reduces the risk of their being blown over.

When using clay pots, in the greenhouse, note that modern greenhouse staging is rarely sufficiently sturdy to take the weight of too many heavy containers. This weight is enormously increased when the soil within has been watered. Staging is mainly designed to support plastic pots, whose main virtue is their cheapness and ability to hold water (which is absorbed by clay).

SEED TRAYS The polypropylene kind are the easiest, being easy to wash and virtually indestructible. Wooden trays used to be popular but they rot, break, and need to be scrubbed hard when cleaned. Yoghurt pots, plastic mushroom boxes and margarine tubs make excellent alternatives.

AUTOMATIC WATERING If you are out a lot use an automatic watering device. They usually involve a tank of water hanging from the greenhouse roof from which plastic tubes leak water into pots or border soil. All you need do is top up the tank.

An alternative is capillary matting which is laid across the staging beneath the plant pots. The tubes leak water onto the mat and the plants draw up all the moisture they require. You can make your own version in which you omit the water bag and tubes, and instead soak the matting each morning.

PLANT CULTIVATION

COMPOST Special compost for pot plants is required because the food content, drainage and oxygenating qualities of garden soil are unsuitable for container plants. The compost tends to be either peat or soil based. The latter are called John Innes and come in three grades, Nos 1-3, depending on whether they have twice or three times as much nutrient as No 1.

Generally, plants in pots up to 10cm/4in take No 1; 10-17cm/4-7in take No 2; and plants in larger containers take No 3. Peat-based composts are not graded in this way; you must read the manufacturer's comments to determine their nutrient value.

FEEDING Compost nutrients last approximately three months before they're used up or washed out. You must therefore replace them with an all-purpose liquid or solid feed over the growing period. Such feed contains a balanced diet of nitrogen (promoting foliage), potassium (for good flowers), and phosphorous (fruit ripening and root development). Provide liquid feed to keep pace with a plant's increasing growing requirements (eg tomatoes); solid, slow-release feed is useful if you are regularly away.

Note, you must only feed during the growing season. If practised at any other time you produce lanky growth and considerably weaken the plant.

POTTING ON When a plant becomes root-bound move up into the next size pot. Remove the plant from its existing container by putting the fingers of one hand across the surface, turning it upside down, and tapping the rim on the work surface. The plant should easily slide out. Cut back any really long roots level with the root-ball and remove some surface compost.

Next put a handful of broken crocks, curved side up, into the bottom of the new container for efficient drainage and fill the sides and top with compost. Finally water in.

POTTING BULBS When dealing with bulbs and corms let them die down naturally after flowering, dry off and rest, and then repot them in the same size container (or one a little larger), with fresh compost. Discard the old compost, and remove withered roots, though only partially if new white ones are evident. They must not, under any circumstances, be damaged.

PROPAGATION

In 99 per cent of cases propagating is child's play. It either involves seed sowing or taking cuttings. Generally, dahlia, delphinium etc, are propagated in early spring allowing the new plants to flower that summer; plants with corms are propagated several weeks later; and geraniums, fuchsias, etc, are increased in late summer so they can root before the winter.

TIP CUTTINGS

These are immature non-flowering shoot tips. Many perennials and sub-shrubs are increased in this way. Make a sharp cut just below a node and remove the bottom pair of leaves before placing the cutting in the rooting medium. Sometimes it is best to take a cutting with a heel, as described below. Soft cuttings take 10-30 days to take root.

SEMI-RIPE CUTTINGS

These are firmer than soft cuttings. They are usually taken in summer and do not need added heat; a cold frame is the best environment. Take a cutting from a healthy side shoot of a shrub, if necessary with a heel (ie attached to a slither of older wood at the base). Cleanly remove the soft tip and the lowest pair of leaves before inserting in the rooting medium. Keep the frame closed and spray on warm days to keep moist. The cutting should make a fine young plant the following spring. Any that have not rooted should be discarded.

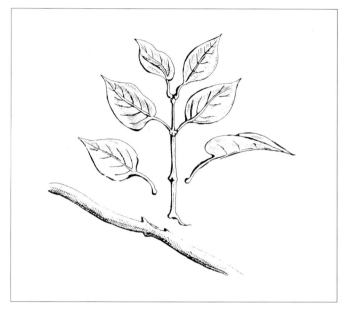

DIVISION

Most perennials are increased by division, and some need dividing from time to time if they become overcrowded. Lift the plant when dormant – between autumn and spring. Separate the sections by hand, trowel or two forks *(above)* in the case of larger plants. Discard the central, woody sections and replant the outer parts. Tough crowns should be washed free of soil and the sections cut up with a sharp knife. Make sure each part has roots and buds before replanting.

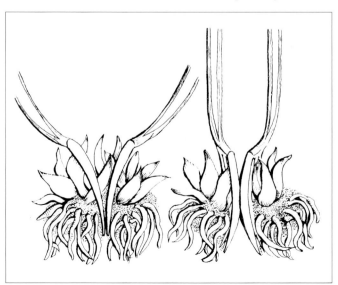

HOW GREENHOUSES DEVELOPED

A graph line tracking greenhouse evolution from Lucius Columella (a first century AD agriculturist who referred to forcing fruit in a 'hothouse' and growing cucumbers in dung pits sheltered by lapis specularis) is initially a weak, spindly curve. It rises at about eight degrees, give or take dips and flips, until lifted by the seventeenth century passion for exotic fruits, John Loudon's 1816 invention of glazed, thin, iron bars, the 1847 introduction of sheet glass and today's mass-produced, easily assembled, streamline shapes.

EARLY EFFORTS John Evelyn (1620-1705), garden designer, writer, friend of Samuel Pepys and adviser to Charles II, is the accredited first user of the word greene house (1664). He was actually referring to a wooden, frost-free house for over-wintering (tender) greens – namely bay, fig, lemon, myrtle, orange, and variegated hollies – which explorers brought back to the UK from the Mediterranean and beyond. Evelyn's diary entry for September 20th, 1700, spells out precisely what these plants had to endure once ashore:

'I went to see Bedington, the antient seate of the Carews ... a noble old structure ... heretofore adorned with ample Gardens, and the first Orange trees that ever were seene in England, planted in the open ground, and secured in Winter onely by a Tabernacle of boards, and stoves, removable in summer...'

These temporary sheds must have been a devil to work with; goodness knows how many plants were lost inside them. Increasingly their contents, grown outdoors in summer in ornamental tubs, were over-wintered in stone or brick structures (orangeries) heated by stoves or fires. Various heating ideas were tried, including hot-air flues beneath floors and inside walls.

SEEING THE LIGHT It was a good job the plants did get five months or so outside because few gardeners

The word greenhouse became part of the English language when John Evelyn referred to a wooden, frost-free house in the seventeeth century. It is thanks to him that several years later, hot air and fumes from stoves were finally replaced with fresh air.

initially appreciated how outrageously bad stove fumes were for plants. Evelyn came to the rescue in 1691 with a greenhouse design eliminating "tainted", 'effete' air, replacing it with fresh. But it wasn't until the nineteenth century that anyone cottoned on to the importance of higher light levels. Consequently in Evelyn's design only the sunny side was glazed, the three walls being solid, the slanting roof laid with tiles. At about the same time there's a description by one J Gibson referring to nine newish greenhouses, four so poorly positioned they barely received any winter sun at all.

Not everyone botched it up though. In the eight-eenth century Dr John Fothergill (1712-1780) created a sensational botanical garden with a 260ft-long greenhouse where he raised orchids. They initially came to the UK in 1732, the first one flowering a year later, quickly becoming collector's items. Other plants were not so lucky, being met by magisterial ignorance of their growing requirements. Everyone assumed tropical plants needed either dampness, a hothouse, jungly environment, or arid desert-like conditions. Anything betwixt was ruled out and plants keeled straight over, ending up on the scrap heap.

Meanwhile wealthy, competitive landowners and nurserymen hired daredevil plant collectors to bring back greater numbers of exotic plants from the world's furthest nooks and crannies. Eighteenth century plant introductions included calceolaria, heliotropium (varieties of), kniphofia, some lilies, lobelia (initially treated as a tender perennial and greenhouse pot plant), *Pulmonaria angustifolia*, *Reseda odorata* (the annual, raspberry-smelling plant from Libya), and *Saxifraga stolonifera*.

Striking Kniphofia *(red hot pokers) make an excellent focal point in the border with their vivid colour and eye-catching height. They are particularly good for coastal gardens.*

Conrad Loddiges was one of the most successful eighteenth and early nineteenth century nurserymen (particularly with orchids). His Hackney garden in London containing 'the best general collection of green-house and hot-house exotics of any commercial garden', with a strong line in camellias, palms, and yuccas. Francis Masson was one of the most successful plant hunters who collected in South Africa, the Azores, and the Canary Islands. He gave us many new pelargoniums and the parent of the modern cineraria, and even created a garden near Cape Town, raising plants for shipment back to England. All anyone now required was a thoroughly decent greenhouse.

It finally arrived in the nineteenth century follow-ing a string of discoveries and inventions. First the appreciation of high light levels led to the glass roof,

13

one of the earliest examples being John Nash's Barnsley Park conservatory (1810). Then in 1815 Sir George Mackenzie hit on the ideal angle of the glass roof, advocating 'the surface of your green house roof should be parallel to the vaulted surface of the heavens, or to the plane of the sun's orbit.'

The following year John Loudon's invention of a wrought iron, curved glazing bar led to brighter domed structures. A cheaper alternative (since it could be made of wood) involved ridge-and-furrow roofs. In 1847 came the invention of plate glass, of uniform thickness, therefore free of the magnifying effects of smaller, uneven panes called Crown glass. The abolition of glass tax (1845) and brick tax (1850) in the UK increased the popularity and spread of greenhouses.

The modern look Greenhouses gradually became a middle-class possession, and the 1840 publication of J Lindley's *Theory of Horticulture* with the subsequent introduction of double glazing, thermometers and hygrometers meant greenhouse gardening became more science than guesswork. That was no bad thing given the way things had been going. In 1817 Loudon went clean off his trolley with a proposal advocating a greenhouse containing a number of artificial climates 'stocked with appropriate birds, fishes and harmless animals, but with examples of the human species from the different countries imitated, habited in their particular costumes and who may serve as gardeners or curators of the different productions.'

A degree more realistic was Joseph Paxton's stupendous Chatsworth greenhouse stove (constructed in 1836 and demolished in 1920). It was so big – 70m/277ft long, 37m/123ft wide, with 7,000 sq m/ 75,000 sq ft of glass – that Queen Victoria drove straight through in an open carriage. The botanical highlight was the giant waterlily *Victoria amazonica*, a table-top of a plant on which a child managed to sit cross-legged. It grew in a 1.2 sq m/12 sq ft tank, just over 1m/3ft 3in deep, on top of five loads of soil dumped in the centre. A small water wheel provided the equivalent of a continuous, gentle current.

The time spent waiting for it to flower was akin to the run-up to the birth of a royal sprogget. Daily the plant swelled, announcements were sent to

John Paxton designed the Conservative Wall in 1848. It is now known as Paxton's Case and one of the great attractions in the 101m/331 ft long greenhouse is the camelia, planted in 1850, plus peaches, apricots and figs.

Chatsworth's owner, the Duke of Devonshire, in Ireland, and then it happened. Around 2pm, November 2nd, 1849, out popped an 'enormous bud like a poppy head' wrote Paxton. 'It looks like a large peach placed in a cup. No words can describe the grandeur and beauty of the plant.'

A second description of Chatsworth comes from one S Hall (who visited in 1851). It was 'filled with the rarest Exotics ... here you see the rich banana, Eschol's grape, hanging in ripe profusion beneath the shadow of immense paper-like leaves; the feathery cocoa palm, with its head peering almost to the lofty arched roof; ... and cassia.'

Heating the 5,058 sq m/1¼ acre interior involved eight boilers enterprisingly linked by 11km/7 miles of pipes to chimneys sited well away from the glasshouse lest their emissions blocked out the light, which is precisely what happened at Dalkeith Palace. (Hot-water pipes were introduced in 1818 when someone twigged that hot water circulated of its own accord. This is still the means used in many long, narrow greenhouses in country house gardens.)

The glasshouse that ranked as a monument to All Industrial Things British – save the fire engine – was Paxton's Crystal Palace which contained the 1851 Great Exhibition and earned him a knighthood. It stood in Hyde Park, was transferred three years later, and went up in flames in 1936. It covered

In 1851, Crystal Palace was the biggest glasshouse on record. Despite the fact that it was criticized by many, it undoubtedly had a stong effect upon domestic greenhouses. In one season it contained a dazzling collection of scarlet pelargoniums and in 1850 it boasted an impressive display of allysum, heliotrope, lobelia and petunia.

7,690 sq m/19 acres, peaked at 30m/100ft high, and used 83,610 sq m/900,000 sq ft of glass (⅓ of the national glass output). It was the biggest glass house on record.

Elm trees previously growing untended out in the open benefited from their new glass environment and regular attention, and thrived. They now made 1.8m/6ft-long shoots against the previous average of 30cm/12in, and prompted a surge of interest in temperate collections instead of tropical ones. In the Crystal Palace – designed to cast 'Versailles into insignificance' – one season's planting scheme ran to 50,000 scarlet pelargoniums, and in 1854 to a collection of alyssum, calceolaria, gaultheria, heliotrope, lobelia, nemophila, petunia, and salvia. But the attempt to out-Versailles Versailles floundered on various distinguished minds.

The spirited Irishman William Robinson – who dispelled 'a general but erroneous idea that the plants of alpine regions cannot be grown in gardens' and reintroduced the secateur – rubbished the Crystal Palace as 'making hideous a fine piece of ground.' Whatever the case, the Palace's wooden construction at Hyde Park was an important influence on domestic greenhouses, though iron yielded finer detail on large-scale, ornate, intricate, curvilinear designs (erected by wealthy landowners). That trend declined with Lascelles's wood-bending steam process of 1874. The Palace was also the forerunner of the glazed exhibition centre, with winter gardens springing up all over the place from the 1860s-90s.

One gigantic glass enclosure that never made it was John Wills's cathedral-like design (1877) to protect the Albert Memorial from pollution. Two that did get built were Kew's Palm, and Temperate Houses (built 1844-48, and 1860).

WILD ARRANGEMENTS The 1860s also saw a radical change in conservatory/greenhouse plant arrangement. Specimens arranged in pots were yesterday's news; in came displays, set in beds, mimicking their native environment. The idea was drummed up by Edouard Andre who wanted visitors to imagine they were out there, in the wild, not inside a gargantuan construction. Hence James Pulham's Poles Park fernery (1865) and waterfalls at Brighton's aquarium (1872).

More ambitious was the packed tropical jungle inside Ascog Hall conservatory and the rockery at Oakworth House. Here natural stone rock faces harboured mini-waterfalls, and an artificial tree contained a staircase. Up people climbed to survey the 'landscape'. To some the designers were bonkers, two currant buns short of a picnic, but their splendid schemes were fun, particularly for anyone too poor to travel and see plants like the 1m/3ft 3in-diameter, barrel-shaped *Echinocactus grusonii* in the wild.

Such creations became too ruinously expensive to build and heat after the First World War. Smaller, cheaper, production-line cold greenhouses came into their own. Today's costs are not beyond most gardeners and with the polythene tunnel and paraffin heater everyone has access to at least a crude, but nonetheless pretty effective, greenhouse. As can be seen from the following entries, a wide range of crops can be grown within them.

NATURAL PREDATORS

Encarsia formosa is a parasitic wasp which lays its eggs in whitefly larvae. The emerging wasps promptly eat their hosts. *Phytoseiulus persimilis* eats red-spider mite. Both predators are commercially available. If you use them note you will not be able to use insecticides. *Cryptolaemus montrouzieri* is an Australian ladybird which preys on mealy bug. The only problem is it's quite capable of eating other ladybirds.

OTHER PROBLEMS

Moss and algae. When growing on the compost this indicates overwatering. Scrape off and in future keep affected plants drier. Also, ensure watering cans are not left full of water since algae develops inside and spreads onto plant compost. When moss/algae appear on the greenhouse glass this indicates prolonged high humidity. Remedy by clearing out the greenhouse and scrubbing down.

Over- and underwatering. In both cases plants put on poor growth, the foliage turns yellow and eventually drops. It is far better to wait for the foliage to wilt slightly, indicating it requires a drink, than to overwater which is the main cause of pot plant failure.

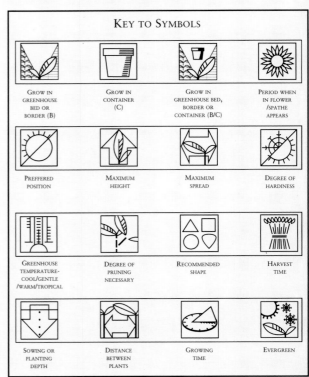

KEY TO SYMBOLS

GROW IN GREENHOUSE BED OR BORDER (B)	GROW IN CONTAINER (C)	GROW IN GREENHOUSE BED, BORDER OR CONTAINER (B/C)	PERIOD WHEN IN FLOWER /SPATHE APPEARS
PREFERRED POSITION	MAXIMUM HEIGHT	MAXIMUM SPREAD	DEGREE OF HARDINESS
GREENHOUSE TEMPERATURE- COOL/GENTLE /WARM/TROPICAL	DEGREE OF PRUNING NECESSARY	RECOMMENDED SHAPE	HARVEST TIME
SOWING OR PLANTING DEPTH	DISTANCE BETWEEN PLANTS	GROWING TIME	EVERGREEN

PESTS AND DISEASES

PESTS

PROBLEM	DAMAGED CAUSED	REMEDY
Aphid (greenfly, blackfly)	Sap sucked; sticky honeydew on leaves	Spray leaves above and below with pirimicarb
Capsid bug	Leaf edges ragged, surface pitted with tiny holes	Spray with systemic insecticide
Caterpillar	Chewed up stems, foliage, flowers	Spray with permethrin or trichlorphon
Eelworm	Weak plants with distorted stems and foliage	Destroy infected plants and discard compost
Leaf hopper	Sap sucked; white mottling/papery white cast-off skins on leaves	Spray with HETP or nicotine. Fumigate with nicotine under glass
Lily beetle	Chewed foliage	Spray with pirimphos-methyl
Mealy bug	Sap sucked; insect evident in white 'wool' covering	Spray with malathion
Red-spider mite	Sap sucked; yellow speckled foliage; brittle leaves	Spray with fenitrothion or malathion. Destroy badly affected plants
Root mealy bug	Root damaged; 'wool' on the inside of the pot	Spray with malathion
Scale insects	Sap sucked; yellow/brown scales on stems and leaf veins	Spray with methylated spirits or malathion
Sciarids	Small grey-black flies that run over top soil of plant pots or fly around them. Damage roots of seedlings and unhealthy plants	Spray with permethrin or malathion
Slugs and snails	Badly chewed up foliage	Bury methiocarb just beneath soil surface in the border. Look for colonies inside empty pots
Tarsonemid mite	Badly misshapen stems and flowers	Destroy infected plants and discard compost. Virtually impossible to treat
Thrips	Silver flecking on leaves and flowers	Spray with fenitrothion
Vine weevil	Entire plant wilts without visible explanation. Caused by black beetles attacking the root system	Discard plant; drench border soil with HCH
Whitefly	Sap sucked; flies clearly evident on foliage	Spray with permethrin
Wireworms	Roots eaten; fleshy seeds attacked	Fork in gamma-BHC

DISEASES

Basal rot	Mainly affects lilies causing stunted growth and root decay	Dip the bulb in benomyl
Begonia tuber rot	Softening of the tuber skin	In future store in warmer, frost-free place
Blackleg	Stem goes soft, shrivelled and black	Destroy infected plants but take cuttings from any healthy remaining growth
Botrytis (grey mould)	Grey fur covers stem and foliage	Immediately remove infected parts. Since botrytis affects damp, badly ventilated greenhouses improve conditions and spray with benomyl
Bud drop	Falling buds caused by too dry an atmosphere or soil, or overwatering	Increase/decrease the watering/humidity
Canker	Rough brown sunken area on stems	Cut out and burn; spray with thiophanate-methyl
Carnation wilt	Leaf yellowing	Destroy infected plants and sterilize the immediate growing area
Club root	Roots attacked, swelling occurs, unpleasant smell; may eventually lead to decay	Alkaline soil and a frequent sprinkling of lime. Water with solution of mercuric chloride or use calomel dust
Cucumber mosaic virus	Often transmitted by aphids and spread on tools. Irregular spots on the leaves and the stem	Destroy infected plants immediately
Damping off	Fungi attacks seedlings causing them to wilt	Sow thinly and water carefully; drench with Chestnut compound
Leaf scorch	Discoloured foliage with brown blotches	Destroy affected areas and spray with zineb
Leaf spots	Brownish blotches and spots appear; leaves shrivel and drop	Spray with mancozeb
Neck rot	Attacks young melons and cucumbers, cacti and succulents	Avoid overwatering. With cacti remove affected parts, eg the top, and re-root.
Oedema	Pimples or warts on the stalks. Outgrowths may become white powdery, blister or turn a rusty-colour	Drier conditions in soil and air. Ventilate greenhouse; do not remove affected leaves
Powdery mildew	White powdery spots on foliage and sometimes stems	Fumigate with dinocap. Remove infected parts
Root rot	Plant wilt caused by overwatering	Transfer to new pot with dry compost and leave for two weeks before watering
Rust	Yellow speckling on upper leaf surface, orange pustules below	Spray with zineb; destroy infected parts; reduce greenhouse humidity
Tomato stem rot	Mature plants begin to wilt. Black patches on the stem	Spray with benomyl

THE COOL GREENHOUSE

5° – 7° CENTIGRADE / 40° – 45° FAHRENHEIT

You take a terrible risk if you don't heat your greenhouse - the first severe winter and the more tender plants will die. Tucked up in clay pots at the back of the greenhouse they are not as safe as you think. The roots are just the width of the pot from encircling, freezing air. They'd probably stand more chance of survival buried under the soil in the open with an insulating mulch on top. At the very least, create warm greenhouse micro climates by placing one plant pot within a larger one, packing the surrounding gap with paper and rags, and covering the soil surface when low temperatures threaten. It's by no means foolproof, but might be worth a go. Better still, use a portable heater for the coldest nights.

With a more sophisticated heating system, guaranteeing the temperature never drops below 5°C/40°F especially from mid-autumn to early summer, you can raise a far greater variety of plants, some from the tropics, and even experiment with the allegedly fussy. Many plants are far hardier and more adaptable than people, or books, imagine. The *Strelitzia reginae* (bird of paradise, *see page 60*) is a good example. Some people grow them in frost-free instead of heated greenhouses. Be warned, this can be a very expensive plant to buy and possibly not worth taking the risk.

PLANT SELECTION
Though most of those in pots will be moved outside from a mild mid-spring to mid-autumn, and won't provide a permanent arrangement, it helps if they look good when together. Aim for a highly varied selection.

ARCHITECTURE Stylish evergreens and shrubs, grown as much for shape as foliage and flowers, provide focal points out of season when not much else is happening. Agaves look stunning all year round with their often variegated, sword-shaped, tooth-edge foliage. Specialist plant centres should have at least eight different species from *A. Americana medio-picta alba* with its dense spikes of bell-like creamy-yellow flowers (similar to the species described *on page 23*, but smaller with more pronounced variegation), to *A. celsii* which grows high in the Mexican forests.

SCENT Fragance is equally crucial; the more rare and unusual the better. *Callistemon citrinus* 'Splendens' foliage, and *Cosmos atrosanguineus* smell of lemon and chocolate respectively, while *Choisya ternata*, most dianthus, hybrid freesias, *Gladiolus callianthus* and hyacinths smell of perfumes that are difficult to pin down and incredibly heady at their best. Stand the choisya in a small greenhouse and the air will be swamped with its scent. Outside, if it's windy for the two weeks when it's in full flower, you won't get anything remotely like the same highly concentrated effect. The pity is it happens but once a year.

FLOWERS If you are passionate about the flowers of one particular species start investigating and comparing its relatives. The plants listed on the following pages are a highly selective group. Societies devoted to many individual genus and plant groups (eg hardy plants) hold their own shows where members

swap seed and cuttings, even ideas on propagating and growing methods. It is well worth visiting the national collections. Above all, remember the plant world is not fixed and finite. Increasing numbers of varieties aren't so much the result of explorers finding what hasn't previously been spotted, but the work of amateurs and high-tech horticulturists creating new hybrids in their greenhouses.

GREENHOUSE MANAGEMENT

It is tempting to imagine that by roasting high-performance plants like scented gladioli, amaryllis and alstroemeria, they will do even better. Not so. On a hot day outside, when it is undoubtedly even hotter under glass, plants in a dry atmosphere quickly transpire and keel over. Shading, humidity, and constant ventilation are essential.

There are many benefits in standing container-grown plants outside, it means you not only minimize the amount of time spent worrying about their growing conditions, but that you also clear the tables for raising seedlings –– flowers, herbs, fruit, vegetables, etc. Yet come autumn you can easily find that new

Alstroemeria ligtu hybrids *sited in an ideal position giving a delightful display of colour*

acquisitions are taking up far more space than imagined and that wall climbers have sailed way beyond their maximum spread. In other words, what went out can't get back in.

If that's the case it's worth seeing if some tenderish plants can survive outdoors. *Callistemon rigidus* is slightly hardier than *C. citrinus* and should be all right in a sheltered position away from extremes of wind and frost. *Osteospermum ecklonis*, buried slightly deeper than usual, should also get by. Don't always look to high protective walls for an answer. They seem far more effective than they are. The prevailing wind swirls up, over and down and can give whatever's in the way a nasty buffeting. Far better is a filtering wall of pines, for instance. In any event, if you are forced to grow the semi-hardy outside over winter, give an insulating protective mulch, site it under or near shrubs, and always take a couple of cuttings for the greenhouse – just in case.

19

PITTOSPORUM

| B/C | summer | sun | 4.5m/15ft | 2.4m/8ft |

Chinese and Australasian evergreen shrubs grown for their fragrant flowers and ornamental foliage. It is risky to put them outdoors and unless the climate is mild, they'll eventually be killed by a bad winter.

GROWING Bright light is essential for good foliage. Plant in rich, free-draining soil, and feed over summer. Trim for shape and to maintain control over rampant growth. Before planting note its size, and that outdoors, given a free run, it's capable of making a substantial hedge.

PROPAGATION Take 7.5cm/3in cuttings in mid-summer. Insert singly into 9cm/3½in pots of John Innes No 1 and raise at a temperature of 20°C/68°F. Leave in their pots until the following spring when they can be planted up into 12.5cm/5in containers

SPECIES *P. daphniphyllum*, from China, has early summer lime green flowers and autumn red berries. *P. tobira (above)* has white flowers turning yellow and a sweet scent. There is also a variegated form.

POSSIBLE PROBLEMS Generally trouble-free.

CHOISYA

| B/C | spring/summer | sun | 1.2m/4ft | 1.2m/4ft |

Choisya, the Mexican orange, can be grown in most gardens given a sheltered position, or better still in ornamental pots and pruned for shape as in the Mediterranean. The small, white, star-shaped flowers open for about two weeks in spring and release the most fantastic scent, sufficient to fill an entire greenhouse.

GROWING Provide well drained soil and John Innes No 3 for large, pot-grown specimens. Stand in full sunlight.

PROPAGATION Easily increase by taking 10cm/4in soft wood cuttings in late summer. Plant in a mix of peat and sand and maintain at 18°C/65°F. Pot up always into the next size container and stand outdoors in summer after hardening off.

VARIETIES *C. ternata (above)* grows to 1.2m/4ft in the open but can be kept smaller in a pot. It has glossy dark green leaves which release a fragrant smell when torn and crushed. *C.t.* 'Sundance' has yellow variegated leaves. Both are capable of flowering intermittently through the summer and again in autumn, but don't count on it.

POSSIBLE PROBLEMS Generally trouble-free.

▧ CUT FLOWER TIP

A great many species of pittosporum have tiny elegant foliage which makes an excellent surround to a flower arrangement. The variegated leaves blend particularly well with the vivid colours and strong scent of freesia, as well as cottage garden carnations.

▧ TOPIARY TIP

Aim for an architectural, swollen-topped mushroom shape to highlight the shiny, dark green scented foliage. Prune when the spring-flowering is over.

PANCRATIUM

C	summer	sun	40cm/16in	25cm/10in

A rare, half-hardy bulb that deserves to be more widely available. It produces scented white flowers with six elegant petals.

GROWING Provide a rich soil, John Innes No 3, with plenty of horticultural grit for good drainage. After autumn planting, water in and increase the following spring as growth appears. Feed regularly over summer and deadhead. As the foliage dies down after flowering cease watering. To protect the bulb in winter it helps if it's grown in a deep pot which can be tucked away in the warmest part of the greenhouse.

PROPAGATION In late autumn separate offsets and pot them up individually. Seed will germinate at 18°C/65°F but don't expect any flowers for at least four years.

SPECIES *P. illyricum* carries clusters of approximately eight star-like flowers on a leafless stem. The flowers of *P. maritimum (above)* are the more fragrant, but they don't always appear in cultivation.

POSSIBLE PROBLEMS Generally trouble-free.

GLADIOLUS

B/C	summer	sun/light shade	1m/3ft 3in	15cm/6in

Most gladioli bulbs are half-hardy and need to be lifted and stored over winter. Some, like *G. callianthus* (also known as *Acidanthera murielae; above*) are particularly refined and highly scented, and are worth growing in greenhouse tubs for an early display.

GROWING Plant corms of *G. c.* in late spring with a 15cm/6in covering of John Innes No 2. The bottom of the pot needs excellent drainage, and each bulb should sit on a sprinkling of horticultural sand. Initially water sparingly and increase with growth. In the autumn, after flowering, decrease watering as the foliage fades. Remove the stems and dry the corms in a cool, well-ventilated spot. Turn them upside down so all moisture can drain away. Store in muslin or netting.

PROPAGATION When the corms are lifted remove offsets and store with the parents. Plant out the following spring. Note offsets can take three years to flower. It is often easier to increase stock by purchasing new bulbs.

VARIETIES *G. c.* has pure white flowers with a purple splash deep inside the trumpet; height 1m/3ft 3in. *G. papilio* has hooded, yellow or white flowers; height 1.2m/4ft. *G. primulinus* also has hooded, creamy-yellow flowers; height 60cm/24in.

POSSIBLE PROBLEMS Core, and dry rot; leaf spot; scab.

▦ GARDENING TIP

It's unlikely that you'll find pancratium in the local garden centre. Far better to try specialist bulb growers. If they don't have it, they'll know who will.

▦ GARDENER'S TIP

One of the most beautiful, hardier gladioli is G. byzantinus. It has rich, magenta-crimson flowers, with three white splashes. Unbeatable.

LITHOPS

| C | late summer/autumn | sun | 2.5cm/1in | 2.5cm/1in |

They don't come any stranger than living stones. Lithops are desert perennials where they only grow for part of the year. They consist of two vertical, fleshy, succulent leaves joined at the bottom but with a split across the top. A white or yellow flower appears from this crack on bright, autumn afternoons.

GROWING Use John Innes No 2 with plenty of grit for free-drainage. Plant in a small pot and leave alone from mid-autumn to mid-spring. No watering is required, and keep the temperature at about 7°C/45°F. The old leaves will wrinkle and shrivel away revealing a new pair. Commence watering only when the new have replaced the old, and cease when they begin to fade.

PROPAGATION Germinate seeds in spring at a temperature of 21°C/70°F. After four years mature plants will form clumps which can then be divided in early summer. Keep dry for 48-hours and then pot up.

SPECIES White flowers: *L. bella* (has dark yellow leaves); *L. fulleri* (beige-yellow leaves). Yellow flowers: *L. dorotheae* (symmetrical green marbling on lime green background); *L. turbiniformis* (brown leaves).

POSSIBLE PROBLEMS Mealy bugs.

ECHEVERIA

| B/C | late summer | sun | 30cm/12in | 30cm/12in |

Olive grey succulents which consist of neat circles of waxy leaves, building up to a 30cm/12in mound in the largest species. In late summer they send up long pole-like stems with flame yellow-orange-red flowers. Eye-catching.

GROWING Start off in small pots with John Innes No 1 and, later, No 2. Free-drainage is essential. Over winter little water is necessary, and when feeding avoid spilling drops into the rosette because they quickly stain. Accidents can be tackled by fiercely blowing away the water. If too many of the plant's lower leaves shrivel and wither, slice off the top in spring and plant up.

PROPAGATION In spring cut away the offsets with a sharp knife. Some may have minuscule root systems. If not it doesn't matter. Dip the soft, fleshy bottom in rooting powder and plant up. It will quickly settle.

SPECIES *E. × derenosa* 'Warfield Wonder' is easily grown, flowering in orange and yellow. *E. derenbergii* has orange flowers and freely produces offsets. *E. setosa*, the Mexican firecracker, is shown above.

POSSIBLE PROBLEMS Beware of overwatering.

■ COLLECTOR'S TIP

Living stones are such peculiar, intriguing plants that most countries have specialist lithop societies. It's worth joining for information on the full range of plants available, fact sheets, and particularly seed supplies of the more unusual species.

■ GARDENER'S TIP

Take outdoors in summer and range along the front of the border. Try them under the dappled light of Cornus controversa 'Variegata'.

AGAVE

| B/C | summer | sun | 5m/16ft 4in | 1.8m/6ft |

Agaves are all about anticipation. It takes up to 20 years for the smaller varieties to produce a beanpole-thin flower stem from the rosette of sword-shaped leaves. In the case of the bigger varieties you may only see the sensational flowering spike twice a lifetime (ie every 30 years). Note the height of 5m/16ft 4in only applies at such times; the bulk of the plant grows to 1.5m/5ft at most.

GROWING Start off young plants in a 9cm/3½in pot filled with John Innes No 2. Place outside over summer but bring indoors in late autumn. Increase the container size when root-bound; otherwise provide fresh soil each spring.

PROPAGATION You can grow new plants from seed, but offsets are far easier. Remove from the parent with a sharp knife and set aside for 48-hours to dry. Pot up in John Innes No 3. They root quite quickly.

SPECIES The spiky and dramatic *A. americana* spreads to a space-demanding 1.5m/5ft. It flowers yellow on a 5m/16ft 4in high stem. *A. filifera* grows to 60cm/24in and has yellow flowers on a 2.4m/8ft stem. *A. victoriae-reginae*, the same height, has white flowers on a 4m/13ft stem.

POSSIBLE PROBLEMS Leaf spot leads to dark blotches on the leaves.

HAWORTHIA

| C | summer | light shade | 15cm/6in | 23cm/9in |

Small, rosette-like succulents with triangular leaves and often warted skin. The bell-like flowers appear on long stems right through the summer, even into the autumn.

GROWING Good pot drainage is crucial. Use sandy loam with plenty of broken crocks and a little sphagnum moss. Over summer place in light shade to avoid leaf scorch. Dry off over winter, but keep the soil moist, and don't let temperatures drop much below 7°C/45°F.

PROPAGATION The simplest method is by division. Slice away any offsets and lay on a tray of sand until roots develop, then plant up.

SPECIES *H. attenuata clariperla (above)* looks like an inverted octopus. It has numerous, vertical, fleshy green stems barnacled with white spots. White flowers commence in late spring. *H. arachnoidea* is a rosette of pointed leaves and also flowers in white. *H. maughanii* eccentrically holds a shield of flat green leaves above the plant and flowers in mid-summer.

POSSIBLE PROBLEMS Mealy bug.

▉ GARDENING TIP

Agaves make invaluable architectural focal points when grown in ornamental pots (maximum size 30cm/12in). Take outdoors in summer and place at the end of a vista, or in the centre of a lawn. The stiff, pointed, tooth-edged leaves contrast particularly well with swirling, cottage garden-type displays.

▉ GARDENER'S TIP

Haworthia can easily be overlooked because they are so small, most are 5cm/2in high, sometimes even less. For best effect grow them in groups of three or four different species, one per pot. Arrange them in front of a larger collection of big, bold cacti.

HYDRANGEA

| C | summer | semi-shade | 1.2m/4ft | 1.2m/4ft |

Hydrangeas are perfectly hardy except in the coldest areas. *H. macrophylla*, in the top league of pot-grown shrubs, has large, colourful balls of flowers consisting of scores of papery florets. The Hortensias *(above)* have sterile flowers while Lacecaps are fertile. The flowers are in shades of purple/blue, white, and pink/red.

GROWING Raise as a small specimen with one large bloom, or as a branching shrub up to 1.2m/4ft high. Give plenty of light and water (dehydration can be fatal, hence the plant's name). Grow in a 20cm/8in pot with John Innes No 2. Blue-flowering varieties require a lime-free compost. Watering with aluminium sulphate keeps the blooms blue and prevents them turning pink/purple which occurs in alkaline soil. Prune the flowering stems in autumn, leaving new shoots for next year's display.

PROPAGATION Take cuttings of 12.5cm/5in long, non-flowering shoots in mid-summer and plant up in a mix of peat and sand. Raise at a temperature of 13°C/55°F, or in a cold frame. Pot up and use John Innes No 2, with growth. Pinch out regularly for shrubby plants.

VARIETIES 'Generale Vicomtesse de Vibraye' has blue flowers. 'Parsifal', red/purple; 'White Wave', white.

POSSIBLE PROBLEMS Generally trouble-free.

FELICIA

| C | summer | sun | 45cm/18in | 45cm/18in |

F. amelloides 'Santa Anita' is the perfect shrubby evergreen for an ornamental pot. It's profusely covered with large, bright blue, daisy-like flowers with yellow centres which close in bad weather.

GROWING Use John Innes No 2 and plenty of horticultural sand for free-drainage. Bring outdoors on warm spring days to harden off but beware of leaving out overnight when there's frost. Prune young plants regularly for bushiness, otherwise they'll become very leggy. Established plants can be nipped back in spring by as much as one third. Beware of over-watering in winter; water liberally and feed throughout the summer.

PROPAGATION Take cuttings of non-flowering new growth in summer and pot up in John Innes No 1. They will put on gentle growth over winter, and will easily fill a 30cm/12in pot by the following autumn.

SPECIES *F. pappei* (also an evergreen) flowers over a slightly longer period, usually into autumn. *F. bergeriana (above)* is a low-growing annual with yellow-centred blue flowers.

POSSIBLE PROBLEMS Generally trouble-free.

■ GARDENER'S TIP

For an earlier display of flowers increase the green-house temperature to 13°C/55°F, and subsequently to 16°C/61°F. For a longer display of blooms force a number of pots at three-week intervals, this also dramatically increases the number of cut and dried flowers for which hydrangeas are renowned.

■ GARDENER'S TIP

F. a. 'Santa Anita' can be brought out of the green-house in late spring, and planted out in the garden border in summer. It forms a substantial bush with *unrestricted root growth and guarantees colour in the mid-summer hiatus between the early flowerers and the late summer bloom.*

SPARAXIS

C	spring	sun	45cm/18in	20cm/8in

There are less than half-a-dozen species of these South African corms, with just a fraction generally available. *S. tricolor*, the harlequin flower, is the most popular. It has vivid red and yellow spring flowers and has spawned many equally brightly coloured hybrids.

GROWING In early autumn group five corms in a 12.5cm/5in pot filled with John Innes No 2. Water in and then wait for growth to appear before continuing. Place outside over summer, in full light, and give a weekly feed. After the flowers and foliage have died down, bring back under glass and dry off.

PROPAGATION The quickest method involves removing offsets in early autumn, when repotting. The problem with sowing seed is that it takes approximately three years before the corm will flower. It's much easier to buy fresh stock as required.

SPECIES *S. elegans* flowers in white or orange while the bloom of *S. grandiflora (above)* is violet-purple. The latter is slightly taller at 35cm/14in, against 20cm/8in.

POSSIBLE PROBLEMS Generally trouble-free.

MIMULUS

B/C	spring-autumn	sun	1.8m/6ft	1.2m/4ft

Grow mimulus, the monkey flower, for strident greenhouse colour – crimsons, sharp-yellows, orange. Some species are herbaceous perennials, preferring permanently damp soil, others make very good pot plants. The taller kinds are perfect for training up a wall or pillar.

GROWING Provide a rich soil, John Innes No 3 with a regular summer feed. In spring repot, and prune for shape and size. Water liberally throughout the summer. Cut back flowering stems in the autumn.

PROPAGATION Take spring and summer cuttings, 10cm/4in long, and raise in a mix of sand and peat. Later move to a small pot of John Innes No 1. Alternatively, germinate seed at 15°C/60°F.

SPECIES *M. glutinosus* grows to 1.8m/6ft and has orange flowers, pink round the lips of the tube; free-flowering. It is sometimes listed as *Diplacus glutinosus*. *M. luteus*, monkey musk, has yellow flowers with maroon blotches. *M. moschatus (above)* is a dwarf species, reaching 25cm/10in.

POSSIBLE PROBLEMS Generally trouble-free.

◼ GARDENER'S TIP

Sparaxis is half-hardy and in a mild climate it may survive under a protective shrub. If you have a plentiful supply of offsets it's worth planting some outdoors and either giving a protective winter covering of bracken, etc, or bringing them indoors to avoid the cold.

◼ GARDENER'S TIP

Mimulus are extremely versatile plants. Grow them in a pot over winter and sink outside in a summer bed wherever you spot a gap or marked absence of colour. On the condition that you don't let the soil dry out mimulus gives instant boldness wherever it is planted.

REBUTIA

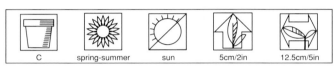

C	spring-summer	sun	5cm/2in	12.5cm/5in

Rebutia is an amazing cactus that produces a mass of flowers around the base of the plant, encircling and almost dwarfing it. Since the cacti are so small it's easy to build up a first-rate collection without sacrificing greenhouse space. Most come from South America.

GROWING Provide a well-lit situation and allow the soil to dry out between watering. In the winter keep it dry, with temperatures no lower than 5°C/45°F. The compost should be John Innes No 2 with liberal additions of horticultural sand for free-drainage. The trumpet-like flowers appear in early summer; they close up at night, re-open the next morning, and last for several days before dying.

PROPAGATION Cut away offsets each spring and plant up. Alternatively germinate seed at 20°C/68°F.

SPECIES *R. deminuta* prolifically flowers in orange. *R. albiflora* develops clusters of elongated cacti with pink-white flowers and yellow centres. *R. kupperiana* produces scarlet flowers, *R. narvaecensis* pale pink, and *R. weingartiana* yellow.

POSSIBLE PROBLEMS Generally trouble-free.

FEROCACTUS

C	summer	full sun	1m/3ft 3in	1m/3ft 3in

Ferocactus have vicious spikes protruding from their colour-ful, round bodies. They flower readily in the wild but not always in cultivation.

GROWING Raise in John Innes No 2, with substantial additions of horticultural sand for the best possible drainage. After each watering wait for the soil to dry out. Cease watering altogether over the winter.

PROPAGATION Increase by seed in spring at 21°C/70°F.

SPECIES *F. acanthodes (above)* has reddish spines and yellow-brown aeroles. *F. hamatacanthus* has red-brown spines and produces pale yellow flowers with red throats. *F. recurvus* is a vertical cylinder with bell-like pink flowers. *F. r. 'Spiralis'* is similar, but has attractive upward-spiralling lines of brown-red spines. *F. robustus* produces yellow-orange flowers and can be propagated by offsets.

POSSIBLE PROBLEMS Mealy bugs; red spider mite.

◾ COLLECTOR'S TIP

R. senilis *is prized for its intriguing spiralling indentation. As the brash red flowers open to either side the feature appears increasingly marked.*

◾ GARDENER'S TIP

Avoid planting ferocactus in the greenhouse border for two reasons. First it detests shade and second, there's every chance a child will inadvertently step on *it. The dense, pointed spikes of the plant will inflict a very nasty injury.*

SARRACENIA

| C | spring | sun | 30cm/12in | 38cm/15in |

An ingenious carnivorous plant which attracts insects to the nectar in its long 'tube'. Unable to escape they are dissolved by various digestive fluids. The pitcher plant is the easiest carnivorous plant to grow, and requires a minimum temperature of 5°C/40°F. They are quite expensive to buy.

GROWING Plant in a special mix of sphagnum and peat which is kept moist with rain or cold, boiled water. Never allow it to dry out for more than 48-hours. Over winter the pitchers die but don't rush to cut them back to the bottom or else they'll promptly lose their food supply. Trim back the tops as they fade. The following spring new growth appears along with weird and curious flowers.

PROPAGATION Divide and re-plant in spring.

SPECIES *S. purpurea* is green with bruise-red mottling. *S. flava* is lime green/yellow with covered tops. There are scores of hybrids including *S. Chelsonii* and *S. Swaneana* which have vivid markings. *S. rubra (above)* has reddish leaves with purple veins.

POSSIBLE PROBLEMS Generally trouble-free.

DIONAEA

| C | evergreen | shade | 12.5cm/5in | 25cm/10in |

The Venus fly trap, *D. muscipula (above)*, is not the easiest plant to keep but it's certainly worth having a go. The insides of the two, fleshy, clam-style leaves are covered with tiny hairs. When an insect pops in, attracted by nectar on the leaf surface and repeatedly brushes the hairs, it sets off a triggered response. The trap shuts and the caught insect is dissolved by digestive fluids. Twenty-four hours later the trap opens and the exoskeleton is blown away by the wind. The plant can flower in the summer.

GROWING Plants are sold in special compost, consisting of peat and fine sand below and sphagnum moss on the surface. Place the pot in a shallow tray of water throughout the growing season. Do not let the temperature fall below 5°C/40°F, and remove the plastic covering that normally comes with the container. High humidity is not necessary.

PROPAGATION The easiest method is to divide an established plant. Ease away offsets and plant up.

VARIETIES This is the only named variety.

POSSIBLE PROBLEMS Generally trouble-free.

◼ COLLECTOR'S TIP

If you want to investigate carnivorous plants seek a specialist supplier and ask for their advice on the best way to start a collection. They'll have a far wider choice of plants than garden centres, and quite often breed their own unusual hybrids.

◼ COLLECTOR'S TIP

A good, starter's collection of insectivorous plants includes giant, fork-leafed, and pygmy sundews; pitcher plants; and bladder-like utricularia.

CHRYSANTHEMUM

B/C	summer/autumn-winter	sun	90cm/36in	75cm/30in

Chrysanthemums are a large group of plants categorized primarily according to their flowering period. The late-flowerers can bloom as late as Christmas. They are grown in pots kept outside over summer and brought under glass in late autumn so the blooms aren't ruined by the frost.

GROWING Container-grown perennials should be potted up in 9cm/3½in pots. Initially water sparingly, giving just enough to prevent the plants from wilting. Later, pinch out the growing tips at least twice for extra bushiness and increase the watering. As the plants put on good growth commence feeding and tie in to a cane. For the final potting up use John Innes No 3. When the plants are brought back into the greenhouse in autumn, ventilate to avoid botrytis.

PROPAGATION When all the flowers have been cut, prune back the stems and store in the greenhouse. Pot up in peat in late winter and increase heat to promote growth. When shoots appear take cuttings 10cm/4in long and root them in seed compost at 16°C/60°F.

VARIETIES There are scores to chose from, including 'Autumn Days' (bronze, early autumn flowering), 'Peter Rowe' (yellow, early autumn), 'Green Satin' (green, late autumn) and the intermediate decorative varieties *(above)*.

POSSIBLE PROBLEMS Earwigs can be a major nuisance.

HYACINTHUS

C	winter/spring	sun	23cm/9in	15cm/6in

All the garden-grown and pot-raised hyacinths are related to *H. orientalis*. The earliest to bloom are the Roman hyacinths (at Christmas), with others flowering into late spring. The fragrance is exquisite.

GROWING Plant mid-winter flowering bulbs in early autumn. Place one in a 10cm/4in pot, or allow 2.5cm/1in between bulbs. Cover to the tip with John Innes No 2 and only lightly press in. Water, place in a dark cupboard, and keep at a temperature of 5°C/40°F. Bring out when there's 2.5cm/1in of growth and gradually increase both light and heat. After flowering, cut off the flowering stem and feed until the foliage fades. Then store the bulbs until the autumn, and plant outside.

PROPAGATION Increase by seed and leave undisturbed until they are at least one year old, then plant up. Note that it can take three years for the bulbs to flower. Offsets are possible but they are rare, and as with seed the quality is not guaranteed. Propagation is best left to the special techniques of professional nurserymen.

VARIETIES 'Delft Blue' is particularly highly scented. 'Jan Boss' is red. 'Lady Derby', pink. 'L'Innocence', white and 'Pink Pearl' *(above)* is deep pink.

POSSIBLE PROBLEMS Grey bulb rot; aphids; storage rot.

■ GARDENER'S TIP

You can force chrysanthemums to flower in two different ways. For a top spray pinch out the central growth leaving behind a cluster of smaller ones. For a single, large, showy bloom remove all buds save for the large one on top of the crown. Carry out all disbudding while the buds are still tiny.

■ SPECIAL CARE TIP

If you plant a hyacinth outside in the wrong place, wait until it's finished flowering before moving it. Move it while in bloom and it promptly keels over.

ALSTROEMERIA

| B/C | summer | sun | 1m/3ft 3in | 1m/3ft 3in |

Sensational South American perennials. Some are fairly hardy like the Ligtu hybrids *(above)*, though they can easily be grown under glass with the more tender species such as *A. pulchella*.

GROWING In early spring sow seeds in John Innes No 1 and pot up 7.5cm/3in seedlings. Provide protection until the following spring when they can be planted out at a depth of 15cm/6in. Established pot plants require John Innes No 2. Water sparingly in spring, but do not allow to dry out, and increase as growth picks up with summer doses of potash. Support the stems with canes and cut back after flowering in late autumn. Repot in spring with fresh compost.

PROPAGATION Lift in the autumn without breaking off the soil round the roots and divide into small clumps. Plant up the tubers in John Innes No 1.

SPECIES Most other kinds of alstroemeria, for example *A. gayana*, 'Margaret', 'Walter Fleming' are frost-hardy.

POSSIBLE PROBLEMS Place pots on the greenhouse staging out of reach of slugs which eat the succulent young stems.

FREESIA

| C | spring/summer | sun | 60cm/24in | 10cm/4in |

F. × kewensis 'Everest' *(above)* is perfect for greenhouse scent and colour. Packets of corms are usually bought as single or double mixed hybrids.

GROWING Plant the corms from autumn to spring, with six per 12.5cm/5in pot, each covered by 2.5cm/1in of John Innes No 2. Insert canes for tying in, and water. Thereafter wait until the foliage starts to grow. Keep pots outside until there's a hint of frost and then bring them under glass and keep at a minimum of 5°C/40°F. Autumn-planted corms should flower the following spring. From the time flowering commences reduce watering to a bare minimum and cut for an indoor vase. When the foliage dies down decrease watering. Keep the corms dry in a cool, bright place until the autumn.

PROPAGATION Freesias propagate themselves at the rate of 2:1 per season. Detach offsets when removing the corms from their pots and that autumn plant up the same-size bulbs together. Offsets may not flower until they've reached a good size in their second year.

VARIETIES Named varieties are usually hard to find.

POSSIBLE PROBLEMS Generally trouble-free.

▦ CUT FLOWER TIP

Alstroemeria make excellent flowers for an elegant, highly colourful spray. Mix with the billowing white star-like flowers of gypsophila.

▦ SPECIAL CARE TIP

Plant corms in fortnightly batches for a continuous display the following year. When cutting them ensure each stem has one open flower and an abundance of swelling buds. They last well in water and the corms should last for years.

OSTEOSPERMUM

| B/C | summer | sun | 90cm/36in | 90cm/36in |

Tender, free-flowering South African daisies which need to be brought under glass over winter except in mild, sheltered gardens. The white flowering, blue-centred *O. ecklonis* is the hardiest and can be left outside in mild gardens, but keep greenhouse cuttings in case it's killed by a very severe winter.

GROWING Pinch out young spring plants otherwise they can become very leggy; the bushier the plant, the more flowers. After the last of the frosts, plant out in full sun and quick-draining soil. Regularly water and deadhead. Container-grown plants put on immense root growth from their second year and need to be checked against becoming pot-bound. In the autumn lift border-grown plants and place in a winter container. You can use a large plastic bucket with drainage holes punched in the bottom. Store in the warmest part of the greenhouse.

PROPAGATION Osteospermum root easily. Take 10cm/4in cuttings of new stem growth in summer and raise in John Innes No 1.

SPECIES 'Buttermilk' is upright, flowering yellow. Pink flowering; 'Cannington Roy' is prostate and 'Chris Brickell' upright.

POSSIBLE PROBLEMS Under glass beware of mildew and botrytis.

CAMELLIA

| B/C | spring/winter | light shade | 1.5m/5ft | 1.2m/4ft |

There's no reason why a camellia shouldn't be grown under glass. Frost-tender varieties won't complain and will provide a far better, earlier display than they would if out in the cold. In addition clever pruning produces a highly architectural plant. Without it, and root pruning, size can be a major problem.

GROWING Feed and water well while in bud. At the same time place pots outdoors, and over summer keep in slight shade. Bring back under cover in late autumn. Always use ericaceous compost when repotting, and rain or cold, boiled water. Camellias will not tolerate calcium, soil that has been allowed to dry out, or roots that are continuously wet. Pots therefore need good drainage material. Regularly deadhead.

PROPAGATION The simplest method is to increase by leaf cuttings in mid-summer. Take a 2.5cm/1in piece of stem with a leaf and bud in the axil, and insert half the length of stem into a mix of sand, soil and peat. Spray regularly with water and raise at a temperature of 13°C/55°F. The alternative method, layering, is far too tricky unless you've got sophisticated, professional equipment.

VARIETIES *C. saluenensis*, spring-flowering in various colours; *C. japonica* flowers early in all shades of pink.

POSSIBLE PROBLEMS Generally trouble-free.

■ SPECIAL CARE TIP

The stems are extremely fragile. When growing in a pot give long, main branches cane support from the start to prevent them being snapped by a heavy downpour. This also avoids a tangled lump and lets light into the centre. If you try to do this later you can easily break off branches heavy with flower buds.

■ SPECIAL CARE TIP

If you have space, an area say 2.1m/7ft by 1.8m/6ft, plant the camellia in the greenhouse border. Ensure the soil is 100 per cent ericaceous and treat as a climbing shrub against the back wall. With its delicate blossom well protected from icy winds you'll be guaranteed Grade 1 results. Ventilate well in summer.

GERBERA

B/C	early summer	sun	38cm/15in	60cm/24in

Gerberas, brightly coloured South African daisies, make exquisite cut flowers. They have a reputation for being difficult, but once you've mastered their likes and dislikes they are no major problem. The plants form a rosette of dandelion-like grey-green leaves, with the flowers popping up on long stalks.

GROWING Provide a warm, sunny spot with little humidity. They particularly dislike root disturbance and dampness. Water sparingly, feed regularly, and avoid potting into too large a container. Pot plants can be brought indoors when they flower.

PROPAGATION The seed germinates well in gentle heat and, if sown early, will produce young plants by mid-summer. They take a couple of years to flower. Alternatively, divide established plants and pot up.

SPECIES *G. jamesonii*, 'Transvaal Daisy', is the most commonly seen plant. It has a circle of red petals with a yellow centre. Dwarf gerberas *(above)*.

POSSIBLE PROBLEMS Aphids.

COSMOS

B/C	summer	sun	60cm/24in	45cm/18in

C. atrosanguineus (above, sometimes known as *Bidens atrosanguineus)* looks good and smells even better. It has a strong scent of chocolate and cocoa. It's well worth growing in a pot or tub.

GROWING Plant the tubers approximately 15cm/6in deep in John Innes No 2. Be patient because growth isn't visible until late spring so don't be tempted to throw them away assuming they're dead. Later, stately, dahlia-like crimson flowers with dark throats appear, and last right through summer to the end of autumn. The stems quickly flop if the soil is allowed to dry out. Bring indoors over winter or, in very mild, frost-free climates, leave outside with a deep protective mulch.

PROPAGATION Increase by dividing the tuber in spring.

VARIETIES There are no named alternatives to this unique Mexican plant. Fortunately it is widely available though surprisingly rarely grown.

POSSIBLE PROBLEMS Generally trouble-free.

▨ CUT FLOWER TIP

Flowers of tall-stemmed varieties can be gathered when fully open. Do not cut in the usual way, but gently pull out the stems as you would a rhubarb.

▨ GARDENER'S TIP

When growing C. atrosanguineus in a large tub surround it with two equally vivid plants. The feathery Bidens ferulifolia is yellow. All are tender and need winter greenhouse protection.

FUCHSIA

| C | summer/autumn | sun | 1.5m/5ft | 90cm/36in |

The first fuchsias were discovered by a missionary in the Americas in 1703. Today there are hundreds of varieties, most of them tender. They can be kept outside through the summer but need to be kept under glass over the winter.

GROWING Younger plants will only survive the winter in a warm greenhouse. Alternatively use a windowsill. In late autumn prune back the main branch by half and water gently in a pot refilled with John Innes No 2. Spray with fungicide to prevent attacks of botrytis. In an unheated greenhouse prune back hard, and reduce watering more significantly. Do not let the soil dry out totally or the plant will die. Provide artificial heat to keep temperatures just above freezing. Recommence regular watering in spring as the plant puts on growth.

PROPAGATION Take young shoot cuttings, 7.5cm/3in long, in spring or summer. Pot up in a 9cm/3½in pot and maintain at 16°C/61°F. Since the best flowers come from young plants take cuttings every other year.

CULTIVARS 'Checkerboard' has bright red and white flowers. 'Dark Eyes', red and violet-blue flowers; 'Lady Kathleen Spence', white and pale pink flowers. 'Thalia' *(above)* has long, red flowers. 'Stanley Cash' is ideal for a hanging basket because it produces a cascade of flowers in white and red.

POSSIBLE PROBLEMS Whitefly; rust.

ERYTHRINA

| B | summer | sun | 1.2m/4ft | 60cm/24in |

E. crista-galli (above), the Brazilian coral tree, is grown outside in mild climate gardens, and is a huge success with its crimson, pea-like flowers above a mass of leafy foliage. It is equally successful under glass.

GROWING Dig well-rotted manure into the bed in the autumn. Plant in the spring and provide good ventilation during hot weather to promote strong shoots and better quality flowers. When the plants are well-rooted, increase the level of watering and feed. After flowering the plant needs to rest so reduce the water supply and keep on the dry side over winter. Prune hard in the autumn.

PROPAGATION Use 7.5cm/3in shoots. In mid-spring insert them into a mix of sand and peat and raise at 21°C/70°F. Pot up as required. A young plant can be hardened off outside over summer.

SPECIES Though there are 100 species *E. crista-galli* is the only one for the greenhouse. *E. c-g.* 'Compacta' is equally free-flowering.

POSSIBLE PROBLEMS Red spider mite can be a terrible nuisance.

■ GARDENER'S TIP

To make a standard take a young plant with a vertical stem. Remove all side branches the moment they appear and concentrate all the plant's energy into upward growth. When it has reached the required height, say 1.2m/4ft, pinch out the tip and allow four side shoots to develop. Support with a cane.

■ GARDENER'S TIP

If there's little spare room in the summer greenhouse, the tree can easily be dug up in the late spring and planted out against a warm, sunny wall.

ABUTILON

| B/C | summer | sun | 3m/10ft | 1.8m/6ft |

The genus includes hardy and half-hardy flowering shrubs which range in size from slender, elegant climbers to small shrubby plants. The tender varieties need frost protection over winter, but should be stood outdoors for the summer. They flower in a good range of bold and subtle colours such as white, yellow, blue, with *A. megapotamicum* 'Variegatum' *(above)* offering green leaves splashed with cream.

GROWING Provide stony, free-draining soil in sunny or dappled shade. If growing in containers use 25cm/10in pots of John Innes No 2. Water generously over summer, sparingly over winter. Floppy stems need to be tied to canes, or against a trellis.

PROPAGATION Take cuttings of 7.5cm/3in side shoots in late spring. Raise in a heated propagator at a temperature of 18°C/65°F.

SPECIES *A. striatum* 'Thompsonii' has mottled variegated leaves and orange bell-like flowers. It'll reach 1.2m/4ft high in a pot. *A. × hybridum* 'Kentish Belle' has similar flowers to *megapotamicum*, but grows slightly smaller at 2.4m/8ft.

POSSIBLE PROBLEMS Whitefly; mealy bugs. It can look pretty wretched over a bad winter.

BELOPERONE

| B/C | summer | light shade | 1m/3ft 3in | 60cm/24in |

Justifiably known as the shrimp plant since that's exactly what the flowers resemble. Incredibly free-flowering in the greenhouse border.

GROWING Place young plants in 7.5cm/3in pots and later repot to a 15cm/6in container. Pinch out the shoot tips regularly for a bushy plant and prune back old or leggy shoots in the spring to maintain shape. For the best flower display ventilate the greenhouse over summer, when a liquid feed should also be given.

PROPAGATION Only use young, unflowered shoots for cuttings. Since they are difficult to find, cut back hard to produce new shoots which can be potted up in late spring.

SPECIES *B. guttata (above)* is now sold under the name *Justicia brandegeana*.

POSSIBLE PROBLEMS Generally trouble-free.

■ SPECIAL CARE TIP

Abutilons like a degree of pampering. Prune straggly growth and remove any brown foliage when repotting in mid-spring. A. megapotamicum *is quite* capable of intermittent flowering through a mild winter, but be sure to remove the flowers when they die since they tend to go mouldy.

■ SPECIAL CARE TIP

Beloperone makes a fine gift as a pot plant but it can lose its shape and get straggly. Move to the greenhouse border and it'll become a dense bush.

DIANTHUS

| B/C | summer | sun | 23cm/9in | 10cm/4in |

While dianthus, or carnations, can easily be grown outdoors certain kinds make excellent greenhouse specimen plants, and are unbeatable for their rich, perfumed fragrance.

GROWING Dwarf varieties can be grown in 13cm/5in pots of John Innes No 2. For tall, stylish specimens plant 12 per grow-bag at a distance of 15cm/6in, or alternatively in individual terracotta pots. Cane support is essential to prevent them flopping over. Only the central bud of each shoot should be allowed to develop if large blooms are required. Water lightly and trim back after flowering to avoid straggly growth. For border carnations pinch out regularly for bushiness.

PROPAGATION Take 10cm/4in cuttings in spring and summer. Pot up into 7.5cm/3in pots of John Innes No 1. Alternatively raise from seed at a temperature of 18°C/65°F.

VARIETIES 'Mrs Sinkins' is a cottage garden favourite. It has white flowers and strong scent. Also good for fragrance are 'Pink Jewel', pink; 'Sops-in-Wine', maroon.

POSSIBLE PROBLEMS Leaf rot in winter.

CALLISTEMON

| B/C | summer | sun | 2.1m/7ft | 1.2m/4ft |

Justifiably known as the bottlebrush tree because it has cylindrical spikes of dense, brightly coloured flowers. Some varieties are hardy in mild areas, but they can be killed off by a severe winter, so keep a cutting in reserve.

GROWING Light and good ventilation over the entire year, not just in summer, are the key ingredients for a successful flowering display. Grow in 30cm/12in pots filled with John Innes No 2 and a good bottom layer of drainage material. During the summer regularly water to prevent the soil from drying out, and give a liquid feed. Repot alternate years and provide fresh compost.

PROPAGATION Take summer semi-ripe cuttings, 10cm/4in long. Raise in a sand and peat mix at a temperature of 18°C/65°F.

SPECIES *C. citrinus* 'Splendens' *(above)* is the most tender kind, and therefore most in need of greenhouse protection. It is an arching bush whose rust coloured leaves turn grey. The crushed leaves smell strongly of lemon. *C. rigidus* is slightly hardier, and has the deeper red flowers. Grown in a bed it can reach 2.1m/7ft, but can be restricted to 1.2m/4ft in a large pot. All are evergreen.

POSSIBLE PROBLEMS Generally trouble-free.

▦ GARDENER'S TIP

It's worthwhile specializing in carnations. Select 20 different varieties and grow them individually in pots. They are highly impressive when lined up on a special table in the greenhouse. Stand outside in groups over summer around a bench where you can fully appreciate the fragrance.

▦ GARDENING TIP

Since a callistemon has good, stiff branches it is perfect for a colourful annual climber to scramble through. Flame coloured nasturtiums are ideal.

ALPINES

| C | early spring | sun | 15cm/6in | 10cm/4in |

Alpines are perfect for unheated, unshaded, extremely well-ventilated greenhouses. The best plants to choose are those that flower in early spring, and those with interesting shaped forms and colours. Seen *above* is *Iris reticulata* 'Harmony', whose planting details are also provided.

GROWING Grow alpines in a gritty, free-draining compost, similar to that used for cacti. Alternatively, make your own alpine compost by mixing John Innes No 1 and horticultural grit, 50-50. If you have sufficient room construct a special table for the alpines on which they can be displayed. Cover it with shingle and bury the alpines up to the rim. Over summer, stand plants outside in a cold frame *(see page 112-13)*. Avoid overwatering at all times.

PROPAGATION Varies according to the genus. The spring-flowering *I. r.* grows from an autumn-planted bulb. Increase by division of offsets one year later.

PLANTS Two good choices are *Pulsatilla vulgaris*, a small fern-like plant with purple, red, pink or white nodding flowers. *Sempervivium arachnoideum* has gorgeous rosettes of green leaves edged red.

POSSIBLE PROBLEMS Protect from slugs and mice, and the damp which is more harmful than the cold.

AGAPANTHUS

| B | summer | sun | 60cm/24in | 60cm/24in |

You may get away with growing the African lily outdoors in a very mild climate, but elsewhere keep under glass. As a guide, note the narrow, strap-leafed varieties are frost-hardy, but not those with broader foliage. The flowers are invariably bright blue trumpets, though hybrids are available in shiny white.

GROWING Outside plant a good 7.5cm/3in below the soil for frost protection, but in the greenhouse border you need not go so deep. Provide a bright situation in rich, free-draining soil. After flowering cut the flowering stems flush with the ground.

PROPAGATION The simplest method involves dividing the plant in the spring. Discard the old, worn-out central clump every few years and replant the younger, more vigorous growth.

SPECIES *A. africanus* is one of the few species that definitely needs greenhouse protection. It flowers in late summer when the dark flowers contrast with the green foliage. Headbourne hybrids *(above)* offer shades of blue, lilac, and cream, and are widely available.

POSSIBLE PROBLEMS Generally trouble-free.

■ GARDENER'S TIP

Stand a miniature dwarf tree among a group of alpines for an extra visual dimension. Salix × boydii is 30cm/12in high, and has delightful grey-green leaves.

■ CUT FLOWER TIP

Gather the seed heads from the long thin flower stems in the autumn and dry. They contrast particularly well with the dried, brown, flower heads of teasel.

GENTLE HEAT

LILIES It helps if you have some plants which can be placed outside over summer, thereby creating extra room inside. Lilies grown in pots are ideal for standing close to a doorway or garden bench because of their terrific looks and, in many cases, heady scent.

To avoid disappointment when buying lilies reject any with damaged skin, brown spots (usually indicative of mould), and soft scales. Nor should you be too impressed with those sold in polythene bags which, if stored in hot conditions, will put on premature growth. Lilies are also prone to a number of pests and diseases. Beware of:

Botrytis leads to wilting and an outbreak of brown spots; remedy with sprayings of benomyl.

Grey bulb rot is evident from a white mould.

Leather jackets gorge on bulb roots and cause rotting.

Lily beetles can badly attack all parts of the flower – stem, foliage, and bloom – and leave behind a disgusting trail of slime.

Since lilies are such astonishing plants it really is worth mastering the basics.

PELARGONIUMS Most cultivated plants bear little resemblance to the real, live, wild thing. Pot-grown ivy-leaved pelargoniums tend to be 30cm/12in high at the most, neatly pruned, tied in, regularly repotted,

trained this way and that. Seen in their native habitat they can grow to a rambling, cascading 4.5m/15ft; zonal pelargoniums grow to 1.5m/5ft. Clearly no-one has that much room to grow pelargoniums big indoors, but in a conservatory or large, heated greenhouse they should just occasionally be given a free run, if only so that we don't totally forget that plants out there are far more vigorous than we imagine.

CLIMBERS One scented greenhouse climber is essential, and though *Jasmine polyanthum* is as common as a winter cold it is still a high-performance plant, easy to grow and easy to flower. The scent from one 45cm/18in plant can easily waft across a medium-size sitting room. Imagine the scent emanating from a 1.5m/5ft climber. If you have room to let it grow to its full potential – approximately 3m/10ft – then plant in the border. If initially grown in a container it'll become pot-bound with enormous regularity and require a good deal of checking and extra work.

Passiflora caerulis, the most popular climbing passion flower, has a distinctive flashy colour combination (white, black, yellow and mauve), protruding filaments, and strong growth. It also gives people a chance to show off, revealing how the ten sepals symbolize the ten apostles, the corona – the crown of thorns, the five stamens – the five wounds, and the three stigma – the three nails. Yet there are other equally showy species which yield edible fruit *(see page 53)*, making them a far more interesting choice.

Another unusual climber is the Brazilian plant *Aristolochia elegans*, the Dutchman's pipe. It has open-mouthed flowers mottled in maroon and white and is usually available from specialist nurseries.

PEST CONTROL The only problem with the gently heated greenhouse, and the introduction of jungly

climbers, is pests. The warmer the conditions the greater the quantity of succulent shoots to feed on; so the more they like it and the more they multiply. Breeding inside starts earlier in the year than outside where it might still be cold, and if there are no natural greenhouse predators you can have a sizeable problem. In addition to introducing the parasitic wasp *Encarsia formosa*, it helps if you occasionally thin out and prune, not merely to keep growth in check, but to keep a close eye on the underside of the foliage.

CACTI Of the thousands of different cacti for the gently heated greenhouse, opuntia are among the stars. They strongly contrast with exuberant greenhouse climbers and keep interest alive right through the year. They have the same growing requirements as any desert cacti. They prefer plastic to clay pots which dry out rather more quickly, and typical cactus compost which is free-draining to avoid waterlogged roots and black rot.

Tempting though it may sound to deprive them of water for long periods, if they go constantly thirsty

There are hundreds of different types of cacti and other succulents which can make a fascinating greenhouse collection. Many of them produce beautiful and exotic looking flowers.

over the growing season they dehydrate. Imitate their desert conditions by drenching them (albeit with added cactus liquid feed) as in a heavy, early morning rainstorm, and then let the soil dry off. A night spray in mid-summer is the equivalent of dew. Over winter, water slightly more frequently than for other cacti.

Being desert plants (and not jungle cacti which have very different requirements, ie higher winter temperatures, more moisture, etc) they need excellent light, without which they will not produce their remarkable flowers. Beware of intense burning sun because it can be too strong and provide good ventilation to avoid the build-up of fungi. Watch out for are aphids, mealy bugs, red spider mite and sciarid flies. Given good growing conditions they should not strike, but you can always water the soil with a precautionary systemic insecticide.

JASMINUM

| C | spring | sun | 1.5m/5ft | 1.2m/4ft |

J. polyanthum (above) is one of the most highly scented indoor plants. It comes from China and can be treated as a 1.5m/5ft climber if given a 30cm/12in pot. In a smaller container, with sensible pruning, it can be kept to more manageable proportions.

GROWING Provide plenty of light. Garden-centre plants often have their stems too closely wrapped round each other. If so, unravel immediately before the task becomes too tricky, and train up and around canes. After flowering in spring cut back to generate new, flowering growth. Over summer stand outside in dappled shade and regularly feed (with additional potash). Bring back under glass in mid-autumn and decrease the amount of watering. Generally, it is better to let the leaves wilt slightly and tell you when water is required rather than to overwater. The cooler the winter/spring temperatures the later will be the flowering.

PROPAGATION Take 10cm/4in heel cuttings in spring or autumn and plant up in a sand/peat mix. Raise at 18°C/65°F over winter and subsequently grow in John Innes No 2.

SPECIES *J. rex* needs higher tropical temperatures and, despite being capable of a much longer flowering period than *J. polyanthum*, is totally scentless.

POSSIBLE PROBLEMS New growth attracts aphids.

PLUMBAGO

| B/C | summer | sun | 5.5m/18ft | 3m/10ft |

Plumbago features one of the all-time Top 10 climbers. The scrambling South African *P. capensis (above)* is thick with sky blue or white flowers in the summer, while the low-growing *P. rosea* has pink-red sprays. Both will grow in gentle heat, but will flower even more abundantly in a warm greenhouse.

GROWING Use rich compost, John Innes No 3, and in the case of *P. c.* train up a strong trellis reaching to the roof. Good sunlight is essential all year round. In winter water sparingly, liberally over summer. Prune hard after flowering to encourage good new shoot production the following spring, on which next year's flowers will appear.

PROPAGATION In spring take non-flowering cuttings, 10cm/4in long, of *P. r.*; summer cuttings are required for *P. c.*. Raise at a temperature of 16°C/61°F in a peat and sand mix.

SPECIES *P. c.* will virtually grow as high as you let it, easily to 5.5m/18ft. In a pot, growth is limited to 1.5m/5ft. *P. r.* is for those short of space – it's maximum height is just 1.2m/4ft.

POSSIBLE PROBLEMS Whitefly gorge themselves on the tender young growth.

■ SPECIAL CARE TIP

Despite good care and attention a small proportion of jasmine leaves and stem growth turns brown and dies over winter. Once a month get out the scissors and give the plant a close check. Snip off dead sections and regularly rotate the pot so all areas are getting plenty of light.

■ SPECIAL CARE TIP

P. c. is a prolific climber and gross feeder. Never let the soil dry out over summer and feed weekly. The more you can provide a humid atmosphere so much the better. And don't worry about keeping the growth too tidy. Plumbago excels when it is a cascade of papery flowers.

LILIUM

| C | summer | dappled sun | 1.5m/5ft | 45cm/18in |

Lilies can be grown in pots or borders. Pots give you greater control over their sometimes fussy growing conditions; you can also move them about, particularly the highly scented. The disadvantage is the extra work. A sane compromise is three extravagant pots.

GROWING In spring, plant three bulbs into a 30cm/12in, deeper-than-average pot. Stem-rooters go in slightly deeper than base-rooting bulbs. Use John Innes No 2, with plenty of horticultural grit and peat, and a thick bottom layer of crocks. First-rate drainage is absolutely essential. Sit the bulbs on a scattering of sharp sand and moisten the soil. Keep in a cool place and when the shoots appear move into the open during the day, but bring under cover while there's still the likelihood of frost. In summer keep the flowers and foliage in the sun, the roots in cooler shade. Let the foliage die down and reduce watering.

PROPAGATION Remove offsets after flowering.

SPECIES For scent; *L. auratum (above)*, white with yellow stripes, though it can be tricky to grow; *L. regale*, white with yellow throat; *L.* 'Pink Perfection', pink; *L.* 'Star Gazer', rosy-red with crimson spots. Unscented; *L.* 'Milano', orange; *L.* 'Yellow Star', golden yellow.

POSSIBLE PROBLEMS Aphids; basal rot; leatherjackets.

CHRYSANTHEMUM

| C | summer-autumn | sun | 1.2m/4ft | 1.2m/4ft |

C. frutescens (above) make excellent, branching, shrub-like plants which are liberally covered with white/pinkish/yellow daisies through the summer, and sometimes up to Christmas under glass. They also have good coverage of fine, and in some cases feathery foliage.

GROWING Plant up in John Innes No 2 and water sparingly over winter. As the plant puts on growth in summer commence feeding. The woody branches tend to become bare at the bottom unless they are pruned back hard in spring to promote soft new growth. Stand outdoors over summer in a heavy pot so they don't get blown over and bring back under cover at the end of autumn.

PROPAGATION In spring remove new growth that does not have a flower bud and plant up in John Innes No 1. It will root without any trouble at 16°C/61°F.

VARIETIES 'Chelsea Girl' has white flowers with yellow centres; 'Jamaica Primrose' and 'Lemon Meringue', yellow flowers; 'Vancouver', bright pink.

POSSIBLE PROBLEMS Without good ventilation, mildew and wilt can strike under glass. Pot-grown plants can be a nuisance, their root systems become so extensive that they fill 30cm/12in containers. Alternatively, plant out in the border over summer before trimming and bringing back under glass.

■ SPECIAL CARE TIP

Bulbs ought to have a good mop of roots when being repotted, but they won't if they've been overwatered the previous autumn. To avoid heavy rainfall after flowering, outside pots should be kept in a sheltered spot, tilted over, or brought back under glass. This gives them a racing start next spring.

■ GARDENER'S TIP

Since cuttings are easily taken it's a good idea to take say six and plant them in ornamental pots. Dotted around the lawn border they give an Italian feel.

39

HEDYCHIUM

| C | late summer | sun | 1.5m/5ft | 1.2m/4ft |

Indian ginger lilies are indispensable for scented gardens. *H. gardnerianum (above)* is the best. It produces spikes of cream-white/yellow flowers with a red filament, and dark green foliage. In mild climates it can be grown outside, given good shelter; otherwise grow in pots under glass.

GROWING Provide a 30cm/12in pot filled with John Innes No 3 and good drainage material. Plant the length of rhizome horizontally in mid-spring and water sparingly at first. During the summer, feed at fortnightly intervals. Stand outside. Cut back flowering stems after the blooms have died; you can leave the foliage.

PROPAGATION When repotting in spring divide up the rhizomes and ensure each section has at least one good, bulging growth bud. Then pot up.

SPECIES *H. coccineum* has red flowers on spikes from mid-summer to early autumn. *H. coronarium* has white flowers with yellow splashes on vertical spikes. Don't let the temperature drop below 10°C/50°F. *H. flavum* has yellow and orange flowers.

POSSIBLE PROBLEMS Generally trouble-free.

CASSIA

| B/C | late summer | sun | 1.8m/6ft | 1.8m/6ft |

The frost-tender South American shrub *C. corymbosa (above)* can reach a massive 1.8m./6ft by 1.8m/6ft outdoors in a mild garden. Fortunately it responds incredibly well to pruning so try growing under glass. The clusters of yellow flowers relish the extra warmth.

GROWING Repot in early spring and increase the amount of watering, particularly during the peak of the growing season. *C. c.* is a vigorous plant whose roots dislike standing in heavy wet soil, so provide good drainage.

PROPAGATION Take soft-wood shoots in spring and plant in John Innes No 1. Alternatively, sow seeds at 24°C/75°F.

SPECIES If you are short of space try *C. alata* which peaks at 90cm/36in high and flowers in winter. Equally compact is *C. sturtii* which has scented blossom. *C. helmsii* from Australia has a distinctly silky appearance.

POSSIBLE PROBLEMS Generally trouble-free.

▓ GARDENER'S TIP

Like heavily scented datura (Brugmansia arborea *and* B. suaveolens) *and lilies (eg* L. auratum, L. regale, *and* 'Star Gazer'), *hedychium is well worth growing in a pot so that you can bring it outdoors on summer evenings and position next to wherever you're sitting.*

▓ GARDENER'S TIP

C. didymobotrya *needs slightly higher minimum temperatures, closer to 13°C/55°F, but the darker yellow flowers will appear off-and-on throughout the year. It's best grown in a pot to restrict growth, otherwise it plumps up to a space-consuming height and width of 2.4m/8ft.*

CESTRUM

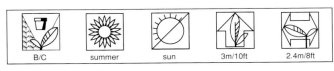

B/C	summer	sun	3m/10ft	2.4m/8ft

A South American shrub which can be grown outdoors in very mild climates, but is generally at its best under cover against a warm and sunny greenhouse wall. It produces extravagant clusters of tubular flowers.

GROWING Provide a rich soil and plant up in mid-spring against a trellis. Cestrum can also be grown in a large tub of John Innes No 3, though it is generally happier in a border. Provide good ventilation over summer and keep the soil moist over winter. Train selected main branches against a wall and nip back side growth.

PROPAGATION Use 10cm/4in cuttings in mid-summer and plant up in a mix of sand and peat. Maintain temperatures of 24°C/75°F, and subsequently pot on using John Innes No 2.

VARIETIES *C. aurantiacum (above)* produces bright orange flowers through the summer, occasionally followed by inedible fruit. Note that at around 7°C/45°F the plant tends to lose its foliage.

POSSIBLE PROBLEMS Under glass whitefly can be a major nuisance. This is less so with container-grown plants when moved outdoors over summer.

OPUNTIA

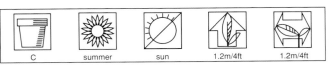

C	summer	sun	1.2m/4ft	1.2m/4ft

Prickly pear cacti are quite a curiosity. They come in all shapes and sizes, ranging from ground cover to trees. They can be as flat as a table tennis bat or bloated. All are sparsely covered with spines, and flower well in yellow or red. Mature plants produce pear-like fruit, edibility varying according to species.

GROWING Unlike many other cacti, opuntia need to be watered over winter and freely in summer. Use John Innes No 2 with plenty of drainage material so the roots aren't continuously sopping wet. Pot up when root-bound.

PROPAGATION Remove recent young growth and leave for 48-hours. Then pot up in John Innes No 2 with additions of sharp sand.

SPECIES *O. colubrina* is rarely seen; growth is in long, narrow, cylindrical joints about 1cm/⅓in thick. *O. echios* has a yellow sheen and yolk-yellow flowers and needs a minimum temperature of 13°C/55°F. *O. pulchella* is clump forming and produces beautiful pink flowers with yellow stamens. *O. stenopetala* 'Riviereana' has flame-orange flowers that turn scarlet. *O. humifusa (above)* has flat, rounded segments and flowers yellow in spring/summer.

POSSIBLE PROBLEMS Mealy bugs.

◼ COLLECTOR'S TIP

C. nocturnum is at its most fragrant at night. Although being very tender it is easily grown from cuttings and is well worth experimenting with.

◼ SPECIAL CARE TIP

Beware the vicious spikes. Opuntia are best grown high up on the greenhouse staging where children in particular won't accidentally trip over them.

CALCEOLARIA

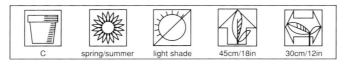

C	spring/summer	light shade	45cm/18in	30cm/12in

The most magical calceolaria have puffed-up, bloated flowers in gaudy colours; sulphur-yellow, blood-red and orange, sometimes with a liberal dash of spots.

GROWING They divide into shrubby and herbaceous kinds. The former are tall specimens and flower for several months. The latter have huge blotched heads, with bright flowers. Shrubby calceolaria will flower profusely in a 15cm/6in pot with John Innes No 2. Induce bushiness by occasionally pinching out. Herbaceous kinds are usually grown from seed *(see below)*. For all calceolaria keep the soil moist and plant in a light, airy position.

PROPAGATION Sow seeds in seed compost and maintain at 18°C/65°F. When large enough to handle pot up singly into a 12.5cm/5in pot with John Innes No 1.

SPECIES C. × *herbeohybrida (above)* has a number of varieties all equally eye-catching. Shades of red, yellow, and orange scream for attention. They tend to be 45cm/18in tall, though there is a dwarf strain, Multiflora Nana, at half the height.

POSSIBLE PROBLEMS Whitefly can be a major nuisance; also leafhoppers.

ASCLEPIAS

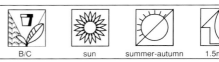

B/C	sun	summer-autumn	1.5m/5ft	1m/3ft 3in

Produces marvellous large seed heads, excellent for a dried flower arrangement, and flowers which butterflies can't resist.

GROWING Plant in a container filled with John Innes No 2 and keep slightly on the dry side over winter. Cut back growth in early spring. When repotting shake off as much old compost as possible. By nipping back shoots in spring the plant bushes out into a fuller specimen.

PROPAGATION Spring cuttings will take root in a propagating frame. Both cuttings and seedlings must be potted off singly once ready, and given larger containers as required. Although a perennial, it can easily be raised from seed and treated as an annual. Seeds should be sown in gentle heat in early spring for flowering later that summer.

SPECIES The two best species for the greenhouse are A. *curassavica (above)*, the blood flower, which grows to 1m/3ft 3in tall and has bright orange flowers. A. *physocarpa* reaches twice that height with a good display of white flowers.

POSSIBLE PROBLEMS Generally trouble-free.

▪ SPECIAL CARE TIP

To grow prize-winning specimens, cool conditions must prevail. Avoid spells of excessive heat and stand the plant in the shade by the greenhouse door.

▪ CUT FLOWER TIP

The dried, large seed heads mix extremely well with contrasting flowering grasses and the puffy, orange fruit of physalis, the Chinese lantern.

LACHENALIA

| C | spring | dappled sun | 30cm/12in | 25cm/10in |

Small, South African, delicate flowering tender perennials which can be grown in pots or hanging baskets. The flowers are invariably striking, tubular, and sometimes mottled.

GROWING Plant the bulbs in late summer, six to a 15cm/6in pot, under 2.5cm/1in of John Innes No 2. After an initial watering, leave alone until the first shoots break surface. Thereafter water increasingly with growth, and feed fortnightly. Shade from the fiercest sun and provide good ventilation. When the foliage yellows and dies down, dry off the bulbs; repot the following summer.

PROPAGATION When repotting remove offset bulbs and pot up, but note they can take several years to flower.

SPECIES *L. aloides (above)* flowers in green, yellow and red. Other varieties include *L. aurea, L. bulbifera, L. quadricolor, L. glaucina, L. luteola,* 'Nelsonii', 'Pearsonii', *L. orchioides,* and *L. vanzyliae. L. g.* and *L. o.* are quite fragrant.

POSSIBLE PROBLEMS Basal rot.

BEGONIA

| C | summer | light shade | 45cm/18in | 30cm/12in |

There are three principal kinds of begonia, the fibrous, the rhizomatous, and tuberous hybrids *(above)*. The latter subdivide into pendulas, cascades, multiflora, and the single-flowering, all of which descend from a handful of colourful South American and Andean species.

GROWING Buy plants in late spring and start the tubers into growth on a warm windowsill. Lay them hollow side up on a tray of moist potting compost. When the shoots appear after four weeks pot each tuber into a 13cm/5in pot, with the tip of the tuber just above the compost surface. Keep in light shade over summer. For show-quality blooms remove the female flowers which are smaller than the large male. Water and feed well. Towards the end of summer, as the leaves yellow, reduce the amount of watering. The flower stems will fall off. Over winter the tuber should be kept in a frost-free place.

PROPAGATION Increase by seed in early spring. Sow thinly and cover with sand. Cover the pot with glass and raise at 18°C/65°F. Transplant seedlings into 2.5cm/1in pots. Alternatively take leaf cuttings.

VARIETIES Tuberous begonias: 'Apricot Delight' has peach flowers; 'Goliath', red; 'Goldilocks', yellow; 'Hawaii', orange; 'Icicle', white; 'Sugar Candy', pink.

POSSIBLE PROBLEMS Aphids; mildew; vine weevil.

■ SPECIAL CARE TIP

Knowing lachenalia comes from South Africa it's tempting to grow it at high temperatures. But don't exceed 7-13°C/45-55°F or lanky growth results.

■ SPECIAL CARE TIP

Since the tuberous begonias' natural habitat is high in the mists of the Andes, spray regularly for humidity to improve the flower quality.

PELARGONIUM

| B/C | summer | sun | 1.8m/6ft | 90cm/36in |

These are not hardy herbaceous geranium but tender, invariably South African plants which survive most maltreatment, except overwatering. This is fatal. The range of plants is huge and increasing annually. Many have scented leaves. It's well worth visiting a national collection to see the latest forms.

GROWING Repot in spring with John Innes No 2, horticultural grit and bottom crocks for good drainage. Pelargoniums can withstand dry soil but not waterlogging which rots the roots. Feed fortnightly over summer and pinch back to increase extra growth. If placing pots of ivy-leaf geranium outdoors, note that heavy downfalls can easily bend and break off the fragile stems. Main branches should be supported and tied in.

PROPAGATION Take cuttings of new growth in summer and root in John Innes No 1. Only when the 5cm/2in pot is root-bound should you pot up.

SPECIES The three major categories are ivy-leaved, regal, and zonal (above), though specialist nurseries offer further kinds. 'Scarlet Unique' is a splendid multi-branching shrub with bright red flowers flecked black. 'Jacky Gould' and 'Rio Grande' (both ivy) are a good mix with papery white, rose-like petals, and red-black.

POSSIBLE PROBLEMS Whitefly.

■ SPECIAL CARE TIP

Fix a 1.2m/4ft cane – with a large wire hoop attached to the top – in a 15cm/6in pot and tie-in a single stem pelargonium to grow vertically up it. Two such pieces of flowering topiary, either side of a doorway, make a stylish feature. Ivy-leaf geraniums will easily reach 2m/6ft 6in given the right conditions.

PRIMULA

| C | winter/spring | sun | 38cm/15in | 50cm/20in |

Many greenhouse primula are natives of China and need winter temperatures of 13°C/55°F. They range in size from the large flowering to the dainty, and are extremely good value.

GROWING Use 13cm/5in pots filled with John Innes No 2 and with good bottom drainage. Keep cool and well-watered while in flower, with some humidity and good light, but out of direct sunlight.

PROPAGATION Germinate seed at 18°C/65°F in early spring. Cover the seed tray with a sheet of glass and remove when seedlings appear. Gradually pot up to 13cm/5in containers, and harden off over summer in a cold frame but again out of direct sunlight. Bring back under glass in mid-autumn and feed with a potash-high fertilizer until the buds begin to open. These primula do not last long (at best several years) and are eventually discarded. Raise fresh stock every other year from seed.

SPECIES P. × kewensis has clusters of bright yellow flowers and a long flowering season. It should last a few years unlike the scented annual P. malacoides which comes in various colours, mainly reds, violets, and white. P. obconica and P. sinensis are equally worth growing.

POSSIBLE PROBLEMS Beware aphids and botrytis in badly ventilated greenhouses.

■ GARDENER'S TIP

All these primula are quite capable of causing nasty skin irritation. To be safe, always handle them with gardening gloves, even as seedlings.

CINERARIA

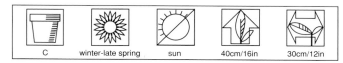

C	winter-late spring	sun	40cm/16in	30cm/12in

Highly attractive winter- and spring-flowering plants, with large single daisy-like blooms in a wide range of colours. Plants are usually on sale from autumn, and last for two months under glass, rather less indoors.

GROWING Treat as biennials, sow this year to flower next, and then discard. Keep mature plants in John Innes No 2 in 17cm/7in pots at approximately 13°C/55°F. As the flower buds swell the temperature can be raised to 16°C/61°F, when feeding commences. Reduce the temperature slightly, as the buds open, and the flowers will last considerably longer.

PROPAGATION Sow the seed from late spring for a Christmas display. Cover the pots with glass and keep moist until they germinate. When four leaves have formed, pot up the strongest seedlings. Gradually move into 11cm/4½in pots using a peat-based soil.

VARIETIES C. cruenta 'Spring Glory' has showy white flowers with a pink outer ring and centre. Other kinds, under the name Senecio × hybridus, come in small and large flowering sizes, in a wide colour range.

POSSIBLE PROBLEMS Greenfly; overwatering.

LIMONIUM

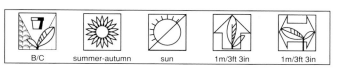

B/C	summer-autumn	sun	1m/3ft 3in	1m/3ft 3in

Sea lavender comes in annual and perennial forms. Both make excellent cut flowers.

GROWING Water gently over winter to keep the roots just moist and repot the following spring. During the summer water liberally, and use free-draining soil with plenty of horticultural grit.

PROPAGATION Increase from cuttings or seed. Take cuttings of new growth (with six leaves) in spring and pot up in a sand and peat mix. Keep at 21°C/70°F and when rooted move into a 7.5cm/3in pot. Reduce the temperature and harden off. Sow the seeds at 16°C/61°F in early autumn for flowering the following summer.

SPECIES Perennials: L. imbricatum, L. macrophyllum, and L. perezii flower in blue. L. sinuatum (above) is covered in abundant pink, blue or white flowers. L. suworowii is lilac-pink.

POSSIBLE PROBLEMS Botrytis, mildew.

■ GARDENER'S TIP

For a year-round flower display repeat sowings in spring (for Christmas), early summer (for winter), and late summer (for the following spring).

■ CUT FLOWER TIP

One of the best for cut flowers is L. latifolium 'Blue Cloud'. The billowing blue flowers, blended with gypsophila, look tremendous in a vase.

NERIUM

| B/C | summer-autumn | sun | 3m/10ft | 3m/10ft |

The main greenhouse species is *N. oleander (above)*. It grows wild in the Mediterranean, and in California is used for high, exuberant flowering hedges.

GROWING Use 30cm/12in size pots filled with John Innes No 2. Place in full sunshine, ventilate, and water liberally through the growing season. Before flowering remove any small growth just below the flower buds or the foliage might cover the flowers. After flowering cut back all flowering stems by two-thirds and reduce the long and straggly stems. Stand pots outside over summer, but bring back under glass soon after.

PROPAGATION Take cuttings of shoots, which will soon grow a good root system in pots filled with a peat and sand mix. Raise at 15°C/60°F.

VARIETIES *N. o. alba* has white flowers; *N. o. splendens* red. Varieties flower in cherry-red, light pink, yellow, apricot and white.

POSSIBLE PROBLEMS Scale insects.

MAURANDIA

| B/C | spring-autumn | sun | 3.6m/12ft | 1.8m/6ft |

A rampant Mexican climber which automatically hangs on to trellis-type support and doesn't need tying-in. (Also listed as asarina.) It flowers right through the growing period.

GROWING Established plants are cut right back in spring, forcing an abundance of strong, new growth. Water gently over winter, liberally over summer. If growing in the greenhouse border add well-rotted manure the previous autumn. Pots are best to restrict growth.

PROPAGATION Early spring cuttings of new shoots root easily in a sand and peat mix. Raise at 18°C/65°F. Alternatively, sow seeds at the same time and temperature, potting them up into small pots filled with John Innes No 1.

SPECIES There are just two from which to select. *M. barclaiana* flowers from mid-spring to late autumn in cherry-mauve and has triangular leaves. *M. erubescens* has furry leaves, a pinker flower with white corolla, and a more triangular leaf.

POSSIBLE PROBLEMS Aphids.

▣ PRUNING TIP

Prune oleander for shape, not quite in the manner of topiary, but for extra elegance. Beware when handling torn leaves, the sap is highly irritating.

▣ GARDENER'S TIP

M. b. is a splendid plant for the edge of a hanging basket. Even though this might mean packing it into a relatively small container with other plants, it still

flowers as profusely as if given a free root-run, and for just as long a period.

LAPAGERIA

| B | summer-autumn | dappled sun | 4.5m/15ft | 1.8m/6ft |

There's only one species of the Chinese bell-flower, *L. rosea* *(above)*. It's got everything but scent. Large, long-lasting, waxy, trumpet-like flowers, and evergreen, heart-shape leaves.

GROWING For best results raise in the greenhouse border, though a 30cm/12in pot will suffice. Use three parts loam and two of fibrous peat with good drainage. If there's any lime present the foliage turns brown and new growth will struggle. Water freely over summer and provide a humid atmosphere with good summer ventilation. If growing in a cold greenhouse mulch the base over winter for protection since temperatures should not dive below 7°C/45°F. Prune only to remove straggly/dead/unproductive growth.

PROPAGATION Seeds germinate at 18°C/65°F. The seedlings need a sheltered place, out of direct sunlight, and should flower in three years.

VARIETIES *L. r.* has rosy-crimson flowers on its twining stems. 'Flesh Pink' is literally flesh pink. 'Nash Court' has large flowers in rosy-pink. There is also 'White Cloud'.

POSSIBLE PROBLEMS Slugs are the main nuisance. They gobble up the tender, young shoots. Also beware of greenfly, thrips, red spider mite and mealy bug.

GREVILLEA

| B/C | evergreen | sun | 2m/6ft 6in | 1.2m/4ft |

This large genus of evergreen trees and shrubs has one major contender for the average greenhouse, *G. robusta*, from New South Wales. It can be grown as a pot plant for its fern-like foliage. It flowers in the wild, but is highly unlikely to do so in cultivation.

GROWING Use John Innes No 2, and keep at 7°C/45°F over winter in dryish soil. Little pruning is required in a 25cm/10in pot. To increase the likelihood of flowering move outside over summer and place in a warm, sheltered spot. *G. banksii* *(above)* has the advantage of spiky flowers in early summer.

PROPAGATION Raise *G. r.* from seed in spring. It will germinate at 21°C/70°F if sown in sandy compost. The large, flat seeds should be placed pointing downwards. Pot up singly when seedlings are large enough to handle. Gradually harden off to the lower greenhouse temperature. Cuttings rarely strike.

SPECIES The half-hardy *G. sulphurea*, reaching the same height, produces clusters of pale yellow flowers in late spring.

POSSIBLE PROBLEMS Generally trouble-free.

▨ SPECIAL CARE TIP

Provide a good, strong trellis, or wires, for the climbers to scramble through. Canes will not hold the weight and will buckle under the strain.

▨ SPECIAL CARE TIP

Avoid planting in chalk-based soil. Use neutral soil instead with large additions of leaf mould incorporated. A loam-based compost is ideal.

ACHIMENES

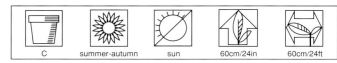

C	summer-autumn	sun	60cm/24in	60cm/24ft

Small, compact, bushy, extravagant flowering plants that 'perform' into early autumn. Despite being popularly known as the hot water plant only give a cool drink. However, you can always occasionally stand a pot of achimenes in a tray of pebbles soaked in warm water. It's the equivalent of giving it a refreshing steam bath.

GROWING Plant the small tuber in mid-spring at a depth of 2.5cm/1in in John Innes No 2. Six can be packed into a 19cm/7.5in pot. Gradually increase the amount of water as the tuber springs to life, and feed over summer every fortnight. Water sparingly through the winter.

PROPAGATION Each tuber increases naturally, by approximately five per annum. Divide in the spring and plant up individually.

SPECIES *A. grandiflora (above)* grows to 60cm/24in and is noticeable for the red colouring under the leaves. The purple flowers are large at 5cm/2in wide. *A. flava* is smaller and flowers in bright yellow. *A. cetoana* is just 23cm/9in high and has violet flowers.

POSSIBLE PROBLEMS Generally trouble-free.

HELIOTROPIUM

C	summer	sun	1.2m/4ft	1.2m/4ft

The most highly scented heliotrope, and the only ones really worth growing, are the old cultivars such as 'Chatsworth' and 'Princess Marina'. They are infinitely superior to modern, poorly scented strains and can usually be found at small, specialist nurseries.

GROWING Let the shrubs take a partial rest in winter when watering can be reduced to a minimum. In early spring remove dead wood and cut back hard all side and straggly branches. When growth begins repot with John Innes No 2 and plenty of drainage material. Regularly pinch out young specimens to achieve a bushy mophead of blue flowers and extra fragrance.

PROPAGATION Increase using cuttings of young shoots preferably in the spring or, possibly, the autumn, in John Innes No 1.

VARIETIES *H. arborescens (above)* forms flat, dense clusters of purple flowers. Also 'Florence Nightingale', 'Lord Roberts', 'President Garfield', 'Princess Marina', and 'Swanley White'.

POSSIBLE PROBLEMS Whitefly can be a major hazard.

▧ GARDENER'S TIP

Achimenes is perfect for a hanging basket. Plant the upright kind in the centre for height, using colourful trailers dotted around the edge.

▧ GARDENER'S TIP

Raise as a standard using a 12.5cm/5in summer cutting. Plant in John Innes No 1 and train up a cane. Remove all side growth until the plant is at a suitable height and then pinch out to force plenty of top growth. It is particularly worth doing this with the scented varieties.

MAMMILLARIA

| C | summer | sun | 25cm/10in | 25cm/10in |

Highly popular cacti which are reliable, prolific flowerers. Shapes tend to be vertical and spherical, with attractive spines.

GROWING Place in a bright place throughout the year, and water carefully. In winter cease watering altogether, in spring water gently, and in summer let the soil dry between liberal applications. The soil, John Innes No 2, should have a 40 per cent addition of horticultural grit to improve drainage. The flowers are mainly white or red, the latter generally appearing later than the former.

PROPAGATION Slice away offsets from the parent in summer and pot up in a mix of four parts John Innes No 1, one part fine sand. Seed germinates at 20°C/68°F. When large enough to handle pot up into 7.5cm/3in pots of John Innes No 2.

SPECIES *M. elegans* send up a long stem with red flowers. *M. erythrosperma* is like a green pin-cushion; cherry-red flowers followed by fruit. *M. sempervivi* has yellow flowers; *M. theresae*, violet-purple flowers; *M. zeilmanniana (above)*, purple flowers.

POSSIBLE PROBLEMS Mealy bugs.

POLYGALA

| B/C | spring-autumn | sun | 1.5m/5ft | 1.5m/5ft |

Of all the hundreds of species, only *P. myrtifolia* 'Grandiflora' is suitable for the greenhouse. It's an ornamental shrubby evergreen from South Africa covered in royal purple flowers.

GROWING In spring prune ruthlessly to avoid leggy growth and promote extra bushiness. Water liberally over summer, particularly if growing in a pot which should be filled with John Innes No 2. Spray during the hottest part of the day, though not when the flowers are in bloom, and ventilate. Over winter, water to keep the soil moist.

PROPAGATION In late spring take heel cuttings of new growth, 10cm/4in long. Raise in a sand and peat mix at a temperature of 16°C/61°F. Keep the soil moist and lightly shaded until the cuttings have rooted.

SPECIES There are various forms of polygala for outdoors, the alpine *P. calcarea* being one of the best. It forms a low mound of blue flowers in the early part of summer. *P. chamaebuxus* has orange-purple flowers, and varieties in dark blue.

POSSIBLE PROBLEMS Whitefly; red spider mite.

◼ COLLECTOR'S TIP

M. blossfeldiana *is the most exotic mammillaria. It has densely packed, white radial spines with black tips, and produces the most beautiful summer* *flowers, 2.5cm/1in radius. They have 11 petals, each white with a central crimson stripe. The stamen is a yellow star.*

◼ GARDENER'S TIP

If you've got a Mediterranean-style garden then grow polygala in a pot under glass and bring outdoors in summer. Mix it with the more willowy P. virgata, *which also has purple flowers, white and pink osteospermum,* Nerium oleander, *and masses of scented thyme.*

CORDYLINE

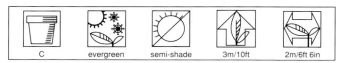

C	evergreen	semi-shade	3m/10ft	2m/6ft 6in

An evergreen shrub or tree with some species unfolding 60cm/24in long foliage. *C. terminalis (above)* is usually raised as a houseplant and grows to 90cm/36in.

GROWING Keep the roots well supplied with water, and spray the foliage freely in hot weather. Wiping them also removes dirt and pests. Some shading and ventilation is necessary during the hottest summer temperatures. Repot in the spring and pot on every alternate year.

PROPAGATION There are five methods. Cut back leggy plants in late spring, remove some of the resultant new growth and use as cuttings. Or, plant up the cut-back stems (say 7.5cm/3in long). You can also break off sections of root and plant up at a temperature of 18°C/65°F. Alternatively, use any suckers. Finally, sow seeds in spring at the above temperature.

SPECIES *C. australis* is slow growing and can be seen outside in mild climates. It also has the potential height of a giant (15m/50ft). *C.a. purpurea* has light-purple foliage. *C. indivisa*, at a potential of one fifth that height, has red streaks on the leaves. All three will flower after seven years or so, if grown in a border, but by that time they're going to need their very own greenhouse.

POSSIBLE PROBLEMS Leaf spot.

ARISTOLOCHIA

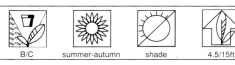

B/C	summer-autumn	shade	4.5/15ft	1.8m/6ft

A collector's item. The climbing flowers are kidney-shaped and hooded, and in *A. elegans*, the best greenhouse species, they are mottled maroon and white. Quite bizarre.

GROWING Likes rich, well drained soil, ie John Innes No 3 with plenty of horticultural sand. Increase water over summer and train up a trellis or network of wires. Prune quite savagely after the flowers have died down to keep growth in check otherwise it will take over the greenhouse.

PROPAGATION Remove 9cm/3½in lengths of stem in early summer and pot up at a temperature of 24°C/75°F. Transfer to John Innes No 2 before giving it No 3 in its final pot size of 23cm/9in.

SPECIES Besides *A. e.* there is *A. gigantea*, a real monster with 15cm/6in flowers and such vigorous growth you'll need a really spacious greenhouse. For cooler greenhouses try the deciduous American native *A. durior* which can even be grown outdoors in the mildest areas.

POSSIBLE PROBLEMS Red spider mite poses the main threat.

▨ GARDENING TIP

The strap-like leaves of C. t. can be woven together and attached to the end of a broom stick. They make an extravagant seaside-style fan.

▨ PROPAGATING TIP

If increasing by seed get them off to a racing start with an overnight soak in a tray of warm water. Then plant in soil at a temperature of 26°C/80°F.

CRYPTANTHUS

| B/C | evergreen | summer shade | 30cm/12in | 35cm/14in |

The nearest plant to a star-fish with radiating, sometimes wrinkly, succulent, multi-coloured leaves. It can be grown in the greenhouse or indoors.

GROWING Plant up in late spring using free-draining soil with additions of sphagnum moss. When feeding use rain or cold, boiled water which is applied sparingly over winter, more liberally through the growing season. Move out of direct, scorching sunlight and into the shade.

PROPAGATION In spring look under the lowest ring of leaves for offsets. Remove with a sharp knife and plant up individually. They should take root fairly quickly and start producing their own offsets within a couple of years.

SPECIES *C. bivittatus (above)* has green pointed leaves with two white stripes running the full length. *C. zonatus* 'Zebrinus' is stranger with mottled, almost hooped green and white wavy lines. *C.* 'Pink Starlight' is the showiest of the group having crimson outer stripes, and a dark centre split by a third red stripe.

POSSIBLE PROBLEMS Generally trouble-free.

LIPPIA

| B/C | mid-summer | sun | 1.5m/5ft | 1.2m/4ft |

Best known for the rich, lemony scent of the torn and crushed foliage. This Chilean climber is particularly good for training up and around a pillar inside the greenhouse. The stems are swathed in hundreds of mauve flowers in mid-summer.

GROWING Plant in spring and commence watering liberally. Cut back established plants to two or three buds, and remove all dead/straggly growth. Place the shrub (or pot) near the greenhouse door to guarantee good ventilation.

PROPAGATION Take spring cuttings of young 10cm/4in shoots with a heel of old wood. Raise in a sand and peat mix and grow at a temperature of 18°C/65°F. When rooted transfer to a 7.5cm/3in pot of John Innes No 1. If growing in the border, plant up the following spring and provide a trellis.

SPECIES Although there are some two hundred species, only *L. citriodora (above)*, or *loysia triphylla*, lemon verbena, is commonly grown.

POSSIBLE PROBLEMS Generally trouble-free.

■ GARDENER'S TIP

Cryptanthus make an intriguing display when planted along the front of the border. You can inject even more interest by alternating them with echeveria which put out 23cm/9in stems in summer with bright red and yellow flowers on the tip. An eye-catching combination.

■ GARDENER'S TIP

The way to get the best use out of lemon verbena is by planting it precisely where you will keep knocking against it and releasing its fragrance.

LUCULIA

| B/C | winter/summer | sun | 3m/10ft | 24m/8ft |

Luculia are rarely grown Himalayan shrubs, some with highly fragrant flowers. The main problem in growing them in the greenhouse is that they are big, and demand much valuable space.

GROWING If raising in a pot use a 30cm/12in size with John Innes No 3. Winter-blooming species should be watered gently after flowering, and pruned hard to promote new growth at the expense of old, straggly stems. Feed fortnightly over summer and water liberally. Container-grown plants need regular repotting.

PROPAGATION Take heel cuttings in summer and raise in a peat and sand mix at 15°C/60°F. Seed germinates at the same temperature but takes several years to flower.

SPECIES *L. grandifolia* has clusters of white flowers in summer, as does *L. pinceana*, though it has got the stronger scent, and is half the height being 1.2m/4ft. *L. gratissima (above)* can reach 1.8m/6ft and has pink/light blue flowers, in winter.

POSSIBLE PROBLEMS Generally trouble-free.

BOUGAINVILLEA

| B/C | summer-autumn | sun | 6m/20ft | 3m/10ft |

A deciduous Brazilian climber theatrically covered in tissue-like bracts surrounding a small flower. *B. glabra (above)* is the ideal species for a greenhouse container and is available in a range of striking colours. Essential in the larger greenhouse.

GROWING Grow in 20cm/8in pots to limit size to 3m/10ft, otherwise it can easily reach 6m/20ft. Use a rich, free-draining soil (John Innes No 3) and water well over the growing period with added liquid feed. In winter keep on the dry side. After the leaves have fallen, give a light pruning to encourage well shaped new growth the following spring. Cane or trellis support is vital. Don't let the winter temperature fall below 7°C/45°F.

PROPAGATION Increase by taking 10cm/4in cuttings in summer and raise at 21°C/70°F.

VARIETIES At least 30 varieties of *B. g.* are commonly available. *B.g* 'Variegata' has white streaked leaves. Other favourites include 'Jamaica Red', 'Orange Glow', 'Royal Purple', and 'Scarlett O'Hara'.

POSSIBLE PROBLEMS Generally trouble-free.

■ SPECIAL CARE TIP

Though lucularia grow robustly and need first-rate conditions, they cannot take direct sunlight on very hot days. Shade for a good flower display.

■ GARDENER'S TIP

The key growing requirement for this native of the Mediterranean, American west coast, etc, is a frost-free winter. Hot summers are not so crucial.

CAMPANULA

| C | summer | sun | 15cm/6in | 45cm/18in |

The most popular greenhouse campanula is *C. isophylla* (above), the Italian bellflower. It has trailing, green-grey, heart-shaped leaves and is available with white or blue flowers. It makes a lively hanging basket.

GROWING Grow in a 13cm/5in pot or hanging basket filled with John Innes No 2. Provide a relatively cool position since it dislikes hot, dry conditions. Keep the soil moist over spring and summer; conversely do not overwater. After flowering, trim back the plant and keep on the dry side through winter at a minimum of 7°C/45°F. The basket can be hung outdoors over summer, but for the best display definitely keep in the greenhouse.

PROPAGATION Take three cuttings 5cm/2in long in mid-spring. Insert in a 9cm/3½in pot filled with loam-based seed compost with a good scattering of fine sand. Campanula rarely fails to take root.

SPECIES As an alternative try growing *C. pyramidalis*, the chimney bellflower, in a pot. It reaches a height of 1.2m/4ft and flowers in late spring. *C. i.* has an attractive variety, 'Mayi', with woolly, variegated leaves.

POSSIBLE PROBLEMS Aphids can be a major nuisance.

PASSIFLORA

| B/C | summer | sun | 7.5m/25ft | 6m/20ft |

The edible fruiting kinds are *P. quadrangularis*, *P. edulis*, *P. ligularis* and *P. molissima*. Other species give outrageously showy flowers. *P. coccinea* is scarlet with a white centre, easily stealing the show from the much-publicized *P. caerulea* (above) with its white, black, yellow and mauve colouration.

GROWING The more rampant species need the free root-run of the border. Otherwise use 30cm/12in pots filled with John Innes No 3. Train up a trellis and regularly water/feed during the growing season. The fruit swell once the flowers have faded and can be eaten when the skin is purplish. Cut in half and scoop out the pulpy flesh. In autumn, as the foliage falls, reduce watering and rest the plant. Later, cut back all stems to 15cm/6in from the soil. Water the following spring as growth appears.

PROPAGATION Use 10cm/4in long cuttings in summer and plant in a peat/sand mix at 18°C/65°F. Transfer seedlings to 7.5cm/3in pots filled with John Innes No 2.

SPECIES *P. edulis* grows to a minimum of 4.5m/15ft, almost certainly higher. *P. ligularia* reaches 7.5m/25ft. *P. mollissima* reaches 6m/20ft and *P. quadrangularis* 7.5m/25ft. All need a winter temperature near 13°C/55°F.

POSSIBLE PROBLEMS Cucumber mosaic virus.

■ GARDENER'S TIP

Two blue and two white cuttings will, if regularly pinched out, quickly fill a hanging basket. If anything, ensure you add a vigorous grower or it'll be swamped.

■ GARDENER'S TIP

If passiflora is too big for the greenhouse you can grow P. caerulea outdoors. Plant against a warm, sunny wall and mulch the top with plenty of straw over winter. New growth should appear the following spring, but take a summer cutting and raise in the greenhouse just in case.

THE WARM HOUSE

13° – 18° CENTIGRADE / 55° – 65° FAHRENHEIT

Higher temperatures mean increasingly exotic possibilities. Plants from Brazil, South Africa, Mexico, and the West Indies can be more easily grown, and the range of tricks gets better.

BIRD IMPRESSIONS Everyone's seen a *Strelitzia reginae* (bird of paradise), but because it's invariably the centre-piece in a sophisticated greenhouse collection, surrounded by exotic, flowering, jungly climbers few bother growing them at home. Actually they're far easier to raise than a *Euphorbia pulcherrima* (poinsettia) which sell by the thousand each Christmas.

Poinsettias *(page 74)* need a fantastically strict daylight regime if they are to flower a second year. Unless you devote yourself to it you might just as well not bother. But with the bird of paradise you needn't even fret about particularly high temperatures. Keep it above 5°C/40°F and the plant sprouts a tufty crest of orange flowers above its prominent green beak. The only possible drawback is size. The bird of paradise

needs a 30cm/12in container; even better a place in the greenhouse border.

Daturas *(see left)* are equally flamboyant. As trees in the wild they grow to the height of a house and are imaginatively decked in summer with look-alike dangling, silky, showy bells. On certain species these beautiful pale coloured flowers emit the scent to beat all scents. Grow them continuously in the heated greenhouse for the best results, and bring them indoors to perfume a room when you're having a dinner party. They won't stand the sudden change in atmosphere for more than a couple of hours, but then they won't suffer irrevocable damage.

Alternatively daturas can be hardened off and grown outside in summer. Some people prefer a continuous cycle. They take late spring cuttings, bring them under glass in winter, plant them out the following summer, and dispense with them that autumn. In very mild climates you can even try leaving them outside all year round. In colder regions you might lose one to the frost eventually, but if you take the view that you've had four year's enjoyment, so what? Simply replace it with a new plant.

The Brazilian tibouchiana can grow to half the height of a datura, but even at 5m/15ft that's still over-the-top. By containing it in a pot you'll restrict growth to 1.2m/4ft and see its tight, swollen red buds, which are nearly as exciting as the purple flowers with a diameter of 7.5cm/3in.

Other star performers include the South American plant, Peruvian *Pachystachys lutea*, whose yolk-yellow flower looks like a plastic lollipop. *Brunfelsia calycina macrantha* produces a flower which does a quick colour change routine. That isn't so unusual since at least two roses perform such a feat. *Rosa* 'Mutabilis' starts off flame-red and ends up crimson, and R. 'Veilchenblau' turns from crimson to lilac-grey. Neither perform quite so fast as this brunfelsia.

FRAMING PLANTS *Hoya carnosa* has a strong woody stem and is easily trained round the inside of the greenhouse doorway. The one irritation is that it takes two years to flower but when it does, you get fist-size clusters of waxy bloom. At 6m/20ft it may be too large for some, in which case *H. australis* (4.5m/15ft) might be better though it's rather more tender and requires a minimum temperature of 15°C/60°F. *Stephanotis floribunda*, Madagascar jasmine, is more manageable at a height of 3m/10ft and has similar flowers, but without the red centre.

SMALL AND COLOURFUL The smaller warm house plants tend to be less scented but extremely good for colour. *Columnea gloriosa*, *Kalanchoe blossfeldiana*, *Saintpaulia ionantha* and *Sinningia reginae* flower in bright red, scarlet, anything from pink to purple, and violet. The advantage of taking your own leaf cuttings of saintpaulia, the African violet, is that you can build up a collection of almost permanently flowering pots. They are quite fussy, and you need to steer a fine line between overwatering and

The bright colours, the beak-shaped bract from which long, blue and orange flowers emerge and the overall striking appearance of the Strelitzia reginae's *flowers, make a fascinating addition to a greenhouse collection.*

high humidity, and bright light and sun scorch. What you are not meant to do though is sell these cuttings. The Plant Varieties and Seeds Act, 1964, guarantees breeders the exclusive right to any profit made from marketing his/her stock.

PLANT HUNTING Most garden centres sell far too few of the wide range of plants that you can raise in the warm house. It's a far better idea to visit the best specialist greenhouse plant collections in the country, note down what you like, and then ask some questions. They will advise on what can be grown in a smaller greenhouse, and spell out the potential problems. With luck, you might even be provided with first-rate cuttings. If not, it should be quite easy to track them down.

HYMENOCALLIS

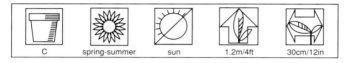

| C | spring-summer | sun | 1.2m/4ft | 30cm/12in |

A genus of perennial bulbs, mainly from South America, with exquisite scent and shape. They have long, thin, curly outer segments like the legs of an elegant white spider. They are sometimes listed as ismene.

GROWING Plant in late winter in John Innes No 2, leaving the bulb's tip just above the soil. By increasing the temperature to just over 15°C/60°F in spring the bulbs will flower early. Water and feed freely up to flowering, and then gradually decrease until the foliage dies down. Barely keep the soil moist over winter for deciduous kinds.

PROPAGATION When repotting in spring remove offsets and pot up. They take at least three years to flower.

SPECIES *H. × macrostephana* is the star choice. It grows to 1.5m/5ft and has white flowers shaded yellow in the centre. *H. narcissiflora (above)*, height 60cm/24in, flowers in spring under glass. *H. × festalis*, height 45cm/18in, flowers in early summer under glass, but not until mid-summer outdoors.

POSSIBLE PROBLEMS Mealy bugs.

CRINUM

| B/C | summer | sun | 60cm/24in | 1m/3ft 3in |

An excellent range of tender, often scented, trumpet-shape bulbs. They are available in strong and subtle shades of white, pink and red.

GROWING Plant up in spring in John Innes No 2 with a deep layer of drainage material at the base. Four are adequate for a 30cm/12in pot. Keep under glass until the last of the frost has passed and temperatures are picking up, and then move outdoors over summer. If the pots are kept inside there'll be an earlier display of flowers.

PROPAGATION The quickest method is by gently removing offsets in early spring but note they can take three years to flower. Seeds sown at 18°C/65°F in John Innes No 1 will easily germinate though they'll take even longer to flower – perhaps five years.

SPECIES In spring *C. asiaticum* has intriguing white, star-like flowers on stems with no leaves. The hardier *C. americanum* has white flowers with good scent in early summer. In late summer *C. × powellii (above)* flowers.

POSSIBLE PROBLEMS Bulb mites.

■ SPECIAL CARE TIP

Only provide fresh soil every alternate year. When not doing so spoon off the top layers and replace with a top dressing of John Innes No 2.

■ SPECIAL CARE TIP

Since the natural habitat of crinum is close to water you could also try growing it in a bog garden. Moist rich soil is the key to success.

STEPHANOTIS

| B/C | spring-autumn | light shade | 3.6m/12ft | 2.7m/9ft |

Stephanotis are like hoyas. Foliage, climbing growth and flowers are all similar. The plants have deep green, fleshy, succulent leaves on woody stems and the scent is rich and powerful.

GROWING Grow in 13cm/5in pots of John Innes No 2 and stand against a firm trellis. Feed fortnightly over summer using a weak feed and since the leaves will easily burn, shade from too hot a sun. Also ventilate and spray for humidity. Beware of letting the soil become too dry in spring and summer or the flower buds will drop. Pot up every spring until you reach a maximum 30cm/12in container when you can also prune to keep growth in check.

PROPAGATION In spring take tip cuttings of mature, not young growth, and insert in John Innes No 1 at 18°C/65°F. Pot up into a 9cm/3½in container.

VARIETIES *S. floribunda (above)* is the one for the greenhouse. Other species are extremely hard to find.

POSSIBLE PROBLEMS Generally trouble-free.

SINNINGIA

| C | early summer/autumn | light shade | 15-25cm/6-10in | 23-30cm/9-12in |

Small, tender, tuberous, summer-flowering plants with velvety or glossy foliage, some of which are listed as gloxinia *(see page 78)*.

GROWING The tubers are started into growth in early spring with a temperature of 21°C/70°F. Pot up into 17cm/7in containers filled with John Innes No 2 in a bright position shaded from scorching sunlight. Give a weak, weekly feed when the flower buds begin to swell and decrease watering with the onset of autumn as the foliage dies. Store the tubers over winter at 15°C/60°F.

PROPAGATION Sow seed and cover with a fine, sieved layer of John Innes No 1. At 21°C/70°F seedlings will sprout up within four weeks. Alternatively, divide the tuber so each section has a strong bud.

SPECIES *S. regina* has heavily white-veined leaves, green above and red below. They contrast with the tubular violet flowers which appear from late spring. *S. eumorpha (above)* has shiny foliage with cream colour flowers flushed yellow within which continue well into early autumn.

POSSIBLE PROBLEMS Root rot.

■ SPECIAL CARE TIP

Stephanotis is a vigorous plant that is best suited to the border. In any event feed regularly over summer for thick sprays of flower and strong scent.

■ SPECIAL CARE TIP

The one thing sinningia dislikes is excess water, around the roots or on the foliage. The latter ruins one of the plants most delightful features.

PACHYSTACHYS

| C | spring-summer | dappled sun | 1.5m/5ft | 1m/3ft 3in |

The two most commonly grown plants are *P. lutea (above)* and *P. coccinea*. The former, also grown as a houseplant, is the Peruvian lollipop plant – so named for its yellow vertical bracts which equally resemble startling, melting candles. The latter needs higher, tropical temperatures.

GROWING Grow in John Innes No 2 in bright conditions, but out of direct sunlight. Water regularly and provide good humidity, keeping the soil on the dry side over winter. Repot each spring when the stems must be cut back to 3.5cm/1½in long to promote new growth.

PROPAGATION The young growth can be used as cuttings, 7.5cm/3in long. Pot up in John Innes No 1 and raise at a temperature of 18°C/65°F.

SPECIES *S. lutea* grows to 75cm/30in and has glossy foliage. The yellow vertical bracts are followed by white blooms. *P. coccinea*, given minimum temperatures of 18°C/65°F, can reach 1.5m/5ft; it has green bracts and red flowers.

POSSIBLE PROBLEMS White fly.

APHELANDRA

| C | summer-autumn | shade | 60cm/24in | 30cm/12in |

The most attractive species have brightly striped green-and-white leaves, out of which grows a four-sided cone with yolk-yellow bracts. A tropical greenhouse is ideal, though you can grow it in these cooler conditions.

GROWING The winter temperature can dip to 13°C/55°F, but from early spring it must rise to 16°C/61°F with an increase in humidity. Old plants can be trimmed into shape at this time by cutting back the shoots which encourages new growth lower down the stem for future flowering. Repot in spring, and give a liquid feed over summer. To preserve the flowers for as long as possible, remove the plants to slightly cooler conditions, but beware of draughts.

PROPAGATION Remove a short length of stem, about 10cm/4in long, and pot up in a propagator at 21°C/70°F.

SPECIES *A. squarrosa* 'Louisae' *(above)*, also known as the Brazilian zebra plant, is the most commonly available and has a showy display of yellow cones and patterned leaves.

POSSIBLE PROBLEMS The plant is particularly prone to blotchy leaves and infestations of scale insects.

◼ GROWING TIP

Pachystachys is such a striking 'look-at-me' plant, it should be stood alone so that nothing detracts from its abundance of flashy yellow bracts.

◼ GARDENER'S TIP

If you like aphelandra but are short on space, try growing the compact variety, 'Dania'. It is just as jazzy as A. s. 'Louisae' but takes up less room.

ALLAMANDA

| B/C | summer | sun | 3m/15ft | 1.8m/6ft |

The genus includes shrubs and climbers but it is only worth bothering with the latter. They certainly take up a lot of room but the best varieties pile up gorgeous yellow flowers. As displays go, this is about the most impressive.

GROWING Rich soil (John Innes No 3) is ideal with a minimum winter temperature of 13°C/55°F. Until spring growth begins, water very sparingly and then commence to liquid feed until early autumn. If climbers get out of hand cut back to the required height, but in any event give support, either along wires or trellis. Flowers appear on new shoots. Regularly check against container plants getting pot-bound.

PROPAGATION Increase by 10cm/4in tip cuttings which have not born flowers in late spring. Raise at a temperature of 24°C/75°F.

SPECIES *A. cathartica (above)* produces sensational yellow trumpet-shaped flowers rightthrough the summer. It can grow to the height of 5m/15ft and if you are lacking in space, try *A. neriifolia* which has smaller but not quite such striking flowers.

POSSIBLE PROBLEMS Generally trouble-free.

THUNBERGIA

| B/C | summer-autumn | sun | 4.5m/15ft | 2.1m/7ft |

Tender climbers, the most popular being *T. alata*, black-eyed Susan *(above)*. Compare it with other species, especially those from India and Africa which are every bit its equal.

GROWING Raise in a 25cm/10in pot filled with John Innes No 2 and place against a section of trellis. Keep the soil barely moist over winter, and increase in summer when a weekly feed is also required. Ventilate and shade on very hot days. *T. a.* can be risked as a half-hardy annual; grow outdoors in mild-climate gardens against a warm, sunny wall. Prune *T. gregorii* hard every spring to prevent it getting out of hand.

PROPAGATION In spring germinate seeds of *T. a.* at 18°C/65°F. *T. grandiflora* can be raised from cuttings, 10cm/4in long, in a peat and sand mix at the same temperature.

SPECIES *T. a.* flowers in orange-yellow with a dark centre from mid-summer to early autumn. It will scramble up to 3m/10ft through the branches of shrubs. *T. grandiflora* has blue flowers and *T. gregorii*'s are plain orange.

POSSIBLE PROBLEMS Generally trouble-free.

▨ GARDENER'S TIP

If you can't maintain the required temperatures, don't worry. Provided the minimum winter temperature doesn't drop below 10°C/50°F the plant won't die and there will still be some flowering, though not as prolifically as with the extra heat.

▨ COLLECTOR'S TIP

Don't be fooled by the species T. fragrans (white flowers). It was misnamed long ago when a batch became contaminated by scented toiletries.

Strelitzia

| B/C | spring | sun | 1.2m/4ft | 1.2m/4ft |

The exotic, intense colouring and flamboyant outline of the bird of paradise, *S. reginae (above)*, suggests it needs very special handling. Not so. In fact the only problem is size. Plants will not flower unless they're in the greenhouse border or a large pot, and easily grow to substantial 1.2m/4ft clumps.

GROWING Use a 30cm/12in pot filled with John Innes No 3 on a thick layer of drainage material. Water gently until the plant is established and maintain a temperature of 13°C/55°F. Increase watering in the summer and decrease over winter. On hot days ventilate, and protect the leaves from scorching sunshine.

PROPAGATION In spring divide mature plants, and raise in a more humid atmosphere at a temperature nearer 18°C/65°F. Alternatively, detach suckers and treat in the same way.

SPECIES *S. r.* is quite different from anything else. *S. nicolai* is a monstrous evergreen, with 1.5m/5ft leaves and a height of 6m/20ft. The flowers, if you can stretch to see them, are pale blue/white.

POSSIBLE PROBLEMS Scale insects.

Guzmania

| C | summer | light shade | 60cm/24in | 60cm/24in |

Epiphytic perennial bromeliads with flamboyantly coloured bracts in yellow, orange, and red. White or yellow flowers appear briefly in mid-summer.

GROWING High temperatures and high humidity are essential to reproduce the tropical conditions of its native South American/West Indian habitat. Provide a rich soil with sphagnum moss and only water with rain or cold, boiled water. Light shade is equally essential.

PROPAGATION Under the lowest circle of leaves tiny offsets will appear. Carefully slice away and plant up in spring. If the offsets are too small wait until mid-summer.

SPECIES *G. lingulata (above)* has crimson bracts, outward-pointing, gleaming green leaves, and yellowish flowers; *G. sanguinea* has yellow-red bracts above dark green leaves. Both grow to 35cm/14in high. *G. vittata* is taller at 60cm/24in.

POSSIBLE PROBLEMS Generally trouble-free.

■ BUYING TIP

Unfortunately S. r. can be very expensive to buy since it takes years for seeds to mature into flowering plants. It's worth tracking down a nursery that *specializes in rare exotica which is prepared to sell them at more reasonable prices otherwise you might end up paying a fortune.*

■ SPECIAL CARE TIP

Since good air circulation is absolutely crucial, avoid growing guzmania in a sheltered greenhouse corner where the air tends to be rather stagnant.

NIDULARIUM

| C | late summer | semi-shade | 50cm/20in | 60cm/24in |

These epiphytic Brazilian bromeliads have sword-like leaves in various shades of green. The bracts turn anything from crimson to light pink at flowering time, and the flowers are invariably in a range of shades from violet to white.

GROWING The compost must be free-draining and therefore incorporate large additions of sharp sand and rough peat. Stand the pot in dappled sun and spray regularly to provide constant humidity, particularly over summer. Water with rain or cold, boiled water but never saturate the compost. Keep it gently moist, and regularly fill the central rosette.

PROPAGATION Ease away the young offsets and pot up. Don't water for at least 48-hours though humidity is essential from the beginning.

SPECIES *N. fulgens (above)* has light green leaves; the white flowers are set off against cherry-red bracts. *N. innocentii* has a spider-like array of leaves; topside olive green, dark red beneath. The bract are flame coloured.

POSSIBLE PROBLEMS Generally trouble-free.

NEOREGELIA

| B/C | summer | semi-shade | 30cm/12in | 30cm/12in |

A particularly bright and cheerful epiphytic bromeliad with strong colours. It is much easier to grow in a pot than strapped to a branch.

GROWING Use John Innes No 2 with large additions of horticultural grit and peat for free-drainage. Spray the surrounding air regularly in summer (weekly in winter) and drip rain or cold, boiled water into the central cup. The soil need only be infrequently moistened, though never allowed to become bone dry.

PROPAGATION When the offsets have developed a root system in mid-summer slice away from the parent and pot up. As with an established plant, water sparingly because too much wet round the roots will rot and kill it.

SPECIES *N. carolinae* 'Tricolor' has green and cream/yellow variegated leaves which flush pink on flowering. The bloom is mauve-purple. *N. concentrica (above)* has violet bracts.

POSSIBLE PROBLEMS Generally trouble-free.

■ SPECIAL CARE TIP

If growing nidularium epiphytically, set it on a damp, stout piece of wood. It not only looks good, but that's how it grows in the wild.

■ SPECIAL CARE TIP

Since it's very difficult to get the right balance between dryish soil and humidity, always remove offsets so you have at least one in reserve. You may *need to raise and lose a number of plants before you master the right approach.*

SAINTPAULIA

| C | mainly summer | light shade | 12.5cm/5in | 23cm/9in |

The African violet, *S. ionantha*, forms a compact rosette of fleshy, hairy leaves out of which flowers appear in a good, strong range of colours. They appear all summer, and often throughout the year.

GROWING Raise in small pots, rarely bigger than 12.5cm/5in, using a peat-based compost. Only water – always from below – when the soil is getting dry, and wipe off any splashes that get on the leaves. This quickly leads to discolouration. Also avoid direct, scorching sunlight. To provide local humidity stand the pot on a tray packed with pebbles and half-filled with water. Over summer feed with weak applications of tomato fertilizer. At 18°C/65°F they should flower freely from summer to autumn, if not beyond.

PROPAGATION Select a mature leaf and cut it off cleanly at the base. Shorten the stem to 4cm/1¾in and dip into rooting powder. Plant in John Innes No 1 leaving a small space between the leaf and the soil surface. It should root in eight weeks.

VARIETIES 'Fancy Pants' has white flowers, edged red. 'Rhapsody' is purple. 'Willy Wilkins' is pink.

POSSIBLE PROBLEMS Tarsonemid mites.

NERINE

| B/C | autumn | sun | 60cm/24in | 23cm/9in |

These South African bulbs can be grown in mild, sheltered gardens but elsewhere will need greenhouse protection. There are several, excellent lily-like forms for the specialist. They are ideal for injecting fresh colour into the mid-summer garden.

GROWING Plant up in 12.5cm/5in pots, with good drainage, in spring. Insert the bulbs in John Innes No 2 which should just cover the tip. Water increasingly with growth and feed at the height of the season. As the foliage fades decrease both, and only recommence the following year.

PROPAGATION The freely produced offsets can be divided from the parent in summer.

SPECIES *N. bowdenii (above)* is the star choice. It has candy-floss, pink, star-like flowers. 'Fenwick's Variety' has even larger flowers; 'Alba' is the white version. *N. b. manina* is a pale pink, while 'Quinton Wells' (possibly a hybrid) is dark mauve. It can grow to 90cm/36in. 'Paula Knight' is blushing pink.

POSSIBLE PROBLEMS Mealy bugs.

▩ PROPAGATING TIP

Instead of increasing stock by leaf, sow seeds at 24°C/75°F. They'll germinate in two months when they can be moved into 7.5cm/3in pots.

▩ GARDENER'S TIP

If you have a big collection of nerine offsets it's worth planting mature spares out in the garden at the foot of a warm wall. They are surprisingly hardy and may survive a bad winter provided plenty of straw is used as a protective mulch. Before they are killed off you should get several years enjoyment.

DIPLADENIA

| B | summer | light shade | 5m/16ft 4in | 4m/13ft |

Easy-to-grow climbers covered in masses of bright, trumpet-like flowers. Some species are scented. All are also listed as mandevilla.

GROWING Plant in a bed rather than a pot, where they rarely succeed after three years. Use soil consisting of three parts loam and one peat, with a sprinkling of sharp sand to improve drainage. Keep dryish over winter and water liberally through summer when ventilation must be increased.

PROPAGATION Increase by side shoot cuttings about 7.5cm/3in long. Insert in pots of sand and raise at a temperature of 18°C/65°F. Pot up when growth begins and the roots have developed.

SPECIES *Mandevilla suaveolens* is a beautiful, deciduous climber with pure white, sweetly scented flowers. It is ideal for trellises and growing under the roof of a large greenhouse. *M. splendens (above)* has crimson-pink flowers with a yellow centre.

POSSIBLE PROBLEMS Red spider mite; whitefly.

DATURA

| B/C | summer | sun | 1.8m/6ft | 90cm/36in |

Datura reach 10m/35ft trees in the wild, sensationally covered in large trumpet-like flowers which give off the headiest scent imaginable. The leaves are hallucinogenic if eaten and cause prolonged outbreaks of vomiting.

GROWING Daturas, or angels trumpets, are vigorous growers. Plant up only to the next size pot, and only when root-bound move up again. Try to limit its growth and height because if you plant straight into a 30cm/12in container the roots will quickly fill it. Use John Innes No 2 initially, and thereafter No 3, and water freely over summer. As the flower buds begin to swell in mid-summer feed with tomato fertilizer. After flowering in the autumn cut back by a third, which also helps to eradicate pests. In a large pot you restrict size to 1.8m/6ft.

PROPAGATION Increase easily by seed. Sow at 18°C/65°F and pot up seedlings into 7.5cm/3in pots. Alternatively, take cuttings of semi-ripe wood in late spring and plant up at 21°C/70°F.

SPECIES *D. arborea* (listed as *Brugmansia aurea*) has white flowers 25cm/10in long, while those of *B. suaveolens* are pale yellow. *D. inoxia* (*D. meteloides*) is the most fragrant of all. For colour chose the apricot *D.* 'Grand Marnier'.

POSSIBLE PROBLEMS Red spider mite; whitefly.

▨ SPECIAL CARE TIP

Leave strong growths alone but cut back weak side shoots to maintain shape in spring. After flowering prune away recent growth if you are short of space.

▨ GARDENER'S TIP

The best way to grow daturas is as standards. Treat in the normal way. Let the stem grow vertically, unbranched, until it reaches 1.2m/4ft.

Then let growth and flowers abundantly break free from the top section only. Stunning when in flower.

CALATHEA

| C | evergreen | light shade | 60cm/24in | 30cm/12in |

Calathea is another very good, very popular, ornamental foliage plant. Most calatheas are equally at home inside a bottle garden.

GROWING Plant up in a rich, free-draining soil in a 12.5cm/5in pot. *C. zebrina (above)*, otherwise known as the zebra plant, needs a slightly larger pot. Use rain or cold, boiled water and keep the soil moist at all times. For the best display of patterned leaves keep the plant sheltered from direct, scorching sunlight and spray in summer. Since calathea is a gross feeder repot with fresh compost in mid-summer.

PROPAGATION In mid-summer use a sharp knife to slice through the tuber. Each segment must have a decent spread of roots and some foliage. Don't let the temperature fall much below 16°C/61°F and pot up.

SPECIES *C. makoyana*, the peacock plant, has showy billowing patches of dark green on a white background with infrequent, short, white flowers. The zebra plant has thick green leaves with symmetrical dark stripes. *C. picturata* 'Argentea', from Brazil, has silver patterning.

POSSIBLE PROBLEMS Generally trouble-free.

PILEA

| C | evergreen | semi-shade | 23cm/9in | 30cm/12in |

Just a handful of the hundreds of pilea are grown in the greenhouse, and *P. cadierei (above)* is the most famous. It's known as the aluminium plant and is grown for the highly patterned foliage with silvery white markings (caused by air bubbles under the leaf surface), rather than its flowers.

GROWING In summer avoid direct sun which yellows and scorches the leaves. In winter give full light and decrease the amount of watering because too damp a soil results in leaf drop. Some humidity is required. Pinch out in spring for extra bushiness.

PROPAGATION Take cuttings from spring on. They should be 10cm/4in long and raised in a sand and peat mix. They root so easily it's worth growing new plants instead of persevering with older, unproductive specimens.

SPECIES *P. involucrata* has brownish leaves with a red tinge beneath. *P. spruceana* has white and bronze foliage.

POSSIBLE PROBLEMS Red spider mite.

■ COLLECTOR'S TIP

Orchid lovers wanting plants for their collection should note the summer-flowering C. crocata. The flowers are orchid-like in orange and red.

■ GARDENER'S TIP

Even though P. c. is the most popular species, P. microphylla is slightly more intriguing. It is known as the artillery plant because from late spring to early autumn when the flowers mature, if you brush a hand against them they are meant to unleash cloudy explosions of pollen.

PLECTRANTHUS

| C | evergreen | sun | 15cm/6in | 15cm/6in |

These evergreens, including *P. oertendahlii*, Swedish ivy, are easily grown and in this case make a fine trailing plant with white-veined, dark green leaves hanging from reddish stems.

GROWING Along with pelargonium, plectranthus are virtually indestructible. Grow in John Innes No 2 and water liberally through the summer, less so over winter. Place in good light, particularly in winter, though it will also tolerate semi-shade. Small, insignificant flowers appear right through the summer.

PROPAGATION Divide in summer, planting up sections which have developed their own root system.

SPECIES *P. australis* has trailing stems and can be used as an edging plant in a hanging basket. The leaves are shiny. *P. coleoides* 'Variegatus' *(above)* is much bushier and has green foliage fringed white.

POSSIBLE PROBLEMS Generally trouble-free.

SENECIO

| B/C | winter | sun | 2.4m/8ft | 1.5m/5ft |

The senecio species for the greenhouse is *S. macroglossus* 'Variegatum' *(above)*. It's a climbing ivy with daisy-like flowers and a reddish stem, and is otherwise known as the wax vine. The pale yellow winter flowers complement the lime green leaf variegation.

GROWING Raise in John Innes No 2 and water sparingly in winter. It is quite tolerant of a warm, dry atmosphere though the occasional misting will greatly perk up the foliage and keep it clean. Growth is on the slow side and sometimes straggly, in which case pinch back for a more manageable, bushier plant.

PROPAGATION Take a 10cm/4in semi-ripe cutting in summer and plant up in John Innes No 1 with additional sharp sand for quick drainage. Pot up the following spring with John Innes No 2 either into a larger container or the greenhouse border.

VARIETIES *S. macroglossus* has plain, mid-green foliage.

POSSIBLE PROBLEMS Generally trouble-free.

■ GARDENER'S TIP

When growing in a hanging basket use the clumps of ornamental foliage as dividers between 'display' plants. This eliminates violent colour clashes.

■ COLLECTOR'S TIP

S. rowleyanus, *string of beads, is a trailing, autumn-flowering, scented plant. It gets its name from the cascading stems, each of which has a collection of* round green 'pearls'. Plant *in a small hanging pot. In a hanging basket with more vigorous plants it easily gets swamped.*

CHLOROPHYTUM

| C | summer | sun | 60cm/24in | 60cm/24in |

The spider plant is at its best when grown into a monster mound of striped, variegated, sword-like leaves lobbing out six or seven 'umbilical' cords with plantlets dangling at the end.

GROWING Although it will tolerate fairly low temperatures of 5°C/40°F, keep at around 16°C/61°F. Give a bright, airy position and use John Innes No 2 for established plants. Repot in spring, water and feed regularly over summer, and watch out for root-bound specimens.

PROPAGATION Place a plantlet onto the surface of a small pot containing John Innes No 1. A piece of hooped wire will keep it in place. Water in, and when it starts to root and put on growth sever from the parent.

VARIETIES *C. elatum* 'Variegatum' is the most popular example. *C. comosum* 'Vittatum' *(above)* has creamy-white bands on the green leaves and flowers occasionally. *C. laxum* 'Variegatum' has more rigid foliage.

POSSIBLE PROBLEMS The leaf ends are invariably brown but there is little you can do about this natural disorder.

PEPEROMIA

| C | evergreen | semi-shade | 90cm/36in | 90cm/36in |

A large group of fleshy plants, mainly from tropical South American rain forests. They naturally grow among tree roots and like to hunt for moisture, not be soaked in it. The flowers don't amount to anything.

GROWING Only *P. obtusifolia* and *P. scandens*, might need pots bigger than 7.5cm/3in. Use John Innes No 1 and rarely water over winter, though the compost should never become bone dry. Use rain or cold, boiled water. During the growing season place in a shady spot and occasionally spray for humidity. Water more regularly but still allow the soil to dry between applications. In winter move to a brighter situation.

PROPAGATION Take cuttings from spring to mid-summer and raise in a peat and sand mix at a temperature of 18°C/65°F.

SPECIES *P. caperata (above)* has dark green leaves patterned with deep wrinkles. The flowers are vertical white spikes. *P. magnoliifolia* has creamy white leaves which mature to pale green. *P. marmorata* has grey-green foliage with deep veining.

POSSIBLE PROBLEMS Eruptions on the leaf are due to oedema.

▨ GARDENER'S TIP

Hang the spider plant pot from the roof of the green-house. The cascading plantlets dangle round the parent, like a sun with satellite planets.

▨ GARDENER'S TIP

P. scandens 'Variegata' is ideal for a hanging basket, though sometimes hard to get going. Its 90cm/36in red stems trail attractive yellow-edged leaves.

SANSEVIERIA

C	evergreen	sun	1.2m/4ft	12.5cm/5in

The most popular species is *S. trifasciata*, mother-in-law's tongue, *(above)*, so named because of the astonishingly long, vertical, indestructible, variegated, wagging, tongue-like leaves.

GROWING Since the plant grows slowly it rarely needs repotting. Use a 15cm/6in pot filled with John Innes No 2 and place in full light to bring out the lime green/yellow edge to the foliage. In the winter if you maintain a temperature of 13°C/55°F, water and allow the soil to dry out between applications. It will certainly tolerate 10°C/50°F if it is kept dry. Give a weak, monthly feed over summer. The plant sometimes produces a green/white summer flower.

PROPAGATION Increase by offsets when they are 10cm/4in tall. Ease them away and pot up in the smallest size container appropriate. Water sparingly at first.

VARIETIES *S. t.* 'Golden Hahnii' has a rosette of dark green leaves, each with broad yellowish borders (height 30cm/12in). 'Hahnii' also has a rosette but with mottled green foliage (height 30cm/12in). 'Laurentii' has vertical, 1.2m/4ft high erect leaves.

POSSIBLE PROBLEMS Brown blotches can appear on the foliage.

DIZYGOTHECA

C	evergreen	light shade	3.6m/12ft	1.8m/6ft

Only one species tends to be sold in garden centres, *D. elegantissima (above)*. It's potentially tall and elegant with spindly, green-grey leaves.

GROWING Provide a rich compost, either John Innes No 2 or 3, and a good mix of sharp sand for quick drainage. Although the minimum temperature is 10°C/50°F it is better suited to hotter, humid conditions.

PROPAGATION Increase by seeds sown in mid-spring at 26°C/80°F. Pot up into 7.5cm/3in pots of John Innes No 1 when large enough to handle. Theoretically you can propagate by cuttings but it's tricky and not worth the bother.

VARIETIES *D. e.* is sometimes listed with *Schefflera elegantissima* which has rounder, glossy green leaves but isn't quite as tall.

POSSIBLE PROBLEMS Generally trouble-free.

▨ PROPAGATING TIP

S. t. 'Laurentii' prefers being propagated by a severed sucker. It is best to wait for four good leaves to develop and then commence potting up.

▨ GARDENER'S TIP

D. e. looks quite dramatic when brought indoors and lit by a floor spotlight. The plant's finger-like leaves cast a maze of shadows on the walls.

CLIVIA

| C | late spring | sun | 45cm/18in | 45cm/18in |

Clivia make excellent choices for rich spring colour. A robust plant can easily produce 40 or more flowers, with different varieties offering bright orange, red and yellow blooms.

GROWING Plant up in 15cm/6in pots filled with John Innes No 2. Be careful with the watering. Over winter make sure the soil doesn't dry out, and through the growing period do not water too liberally. All container-grown specimens must sit above a good layer of drainage material so the roots don't stand in wet soil. The plant will need to be in a 30cm/12in pot within a couple of years .

PROPAGATION To prevent potting up into ever larger containers remove a pot-bound specimen and divide. Transplant the new growth into 10cm/4in pots filled with John Innes No 1.

SPECIES *C. miniata (above)* produces 15 dark orange flowers per stem set against deep green foliage. For variegated leaves chose *C. m.* 'Striata'. *C. nobilis*'s flowers are more of a fiery orange red.

POSSIBLE PROBLEMS Mealy bugs are the main problem.

HIPPEASTRUM

| C | winter/spring | sun | 60cm/24in | 15cm/6in |

Hippeastrum, or amaryllis as it is popularly known, is a vigorous flowering bulb. For very little effort you get a tall, showy display in the first part of the year. Most bulb specialists will have at least 15 varieties to chose from, including one or two with scent.

GROWING In spring plant the bulb half-in and half-out of John Innes No 2. Use a pot just 5cm/2in wider than the bulb's diameter, with plenty of drainage material in the bottom. Wet the soil initially, only increasing the amounts as the temperature rises from 13°C/55°F and growth develops. Delay feeding until two weeks before flowering, but continue thereafter every 10 days until the foliage turns yellow and begins to die. Rest the bulb from late autumn and start it into growth again when it suits you, even as early as late winter. Repot with fresh compost.

PROPAGATION Sow seed in the spring at 18°C/65°F, but avoid resting the growing plants.

VARIETIES 'Apple Blossom' is white and pink, and has mild scent. 'Bouquet' is light pink. 'Yellow Pioneer' is yellow.

POSSIBLE PROBLEMS Mealy bugs; tarsonemid mite; thrips.

▪ PROPAGATING TIP

Don't increase by seed since it can take six years for plants to flower. Instead propagate by division: it takes two years for a brilliant display.

▪ SPECIAL CARE TIP

As growth increases in spring and the flower spike begins to emerge, start increasing the temperature to 16°C/61°F or more. But, after the flowers have *opened, slightly reduce the temperature in order to prolong the flower display.*

BOUVARDIA

| C | summer-autumn | light shade | 1m/3ft | 60cm/2ft |

Bouvardia has a reputation for being difficult to keep, but the strong flower display easily makes it well worth the effort. Flowers over a long summer-autumn period; some species even keep going until Christmas with vivid, scented flowers.

GROWING Prune hard each spring to within 23cm/9in of the base to promote plenty of new growth and repot in John Innes No 2. Water freely over the growing season. Shade from direct sunlight and create a humid atmosphere.

PROPAGATION Increase by young shoots 8cm/3.2in long. Root in a temperature of 21°C/70°F using a peat and sand compost.

SPECIES *B. jasminiflora* has fragrant white flowers; *B. ternifolia* has outward-pointing, tubular, orange-scarlet flowers. *B. longiflora*, from Mexico, has glossy leaves with white scented flowers appearing from mid-autumn until several weeks before Christmas. *B. × domestica (above)* has clusters of red, pink or white flowers appearing from early summer to early winter.

POSSIBLE PROBLEMS Prone to attack from scale insects and mealy bugs.

COLUMNEA

| C | winter-spring | summer shade | 1.2m/4ft | 1.2m/4ft |

An outright winner and a must for hanging baskets. Columnea produces a trailing profusion of tubular, hooded, orange-red flowers.

GROWING Line the basket with moss and fill with good, open compost, either loam- or peat-based, and drainage material. The roots dislike cold, wet soil. Water liberally over summer and beware of root-bound containers. Invariably the trailing plants become bare at the tip of the stems, in which case cut back hard after flowering.

PROPAGATION Use the 7.5cm/3in tip cuttings to increase the supply of plants. Raise in a sandy compost at a temperature of 21°C/70°F. The following spring pinch out to increase bushiness.

SPECIES Over winter/early spring *C. gloriosa* has 1m/3ft 3in trailing stems, and fiery red flowers with yellow shading in the throat. *C. microphylla* has a similar habit, but with smaller leaves. *C. m.* 'Tricolor' has variegated foliage. *C. × banksii (above)* has glossy foliage and orange-red flowers. In summer *C. schiedeana* flowers.

POSSIBLE PROBLEMS Generally trouble-free.

▨ GARDENER'S TIP

For the very best flowering display on the winter-blossoming plants pinch out the shoots right through summer. It makes a sensational difference.

▨ PLANTING TIP

To give the plants vital extra warmth and humidity, plant them really close together. Don't worry about overcrowding; they prefer it that way.

69

SMITHIANTHA

| C | early summer | sun | 90cm/36in | 90cm/36in |

Two Mexican species, *S. cinnabarina* and *S. multiflora*, have produced a wide range of brightly coloured hybrids. All are easily grown from rhizomes.

GROWING In spring place two or three rhizomes in a 15cm/6in pot, cover with 2.5cm/1in of compost, and raise at 18°C/65°F. When in full growth water liberally and give a weekly feed. Also provide a humid atmosphere but do not spray the hairy leaves which easily discolour. When the flowers have faded, and the foliage dies down, decrease the watering and keep the compost dry over winter.

PROPAGATION The rhizomes can be split into 7.5cm/3in sections in spring, each having a strong bud. Alternatively, take cuttings of young shoots and root them in a sand and peat mix at 18°C/65°F.

SPECIES *S. cinnabarina*, Temple Bells *(above)*, has red foxglove-like flowers, flame coloured on the inside; height 60cm/24in. The foliage is purple-green. *S. zebrina* is a little taller and has crimson flowers, yellow within. The hybrids 'Carmello', 'Harecroft', 'Meadowscroft', 'New Yellow Hybrid', 'Pink Lady', 'Summer Sunshine', etc – come in a wide range of bright colours.

POSSIBLE PROBLEMS Generally trouble-free.

KOHLERIA

| C | summer | light shade | 60cm/24in | 60cm/24in |

The flowers often resemble foxgloves, hence one species called *K. digitaliflora*. High, near tropical temperatures are required in return for which the plant is free-flowering and easily propagated.

GROWING Force the rhizome into growth in late winter at 18°C/65°F in a small pot. Water with increasing frequency as growth increases and pot up only when root-bound. Summer feed, light shade and humidity are essential, the latter particularly on hot days. Dry off as the foliage dies down and keep at 13°C/55°F over winter. Discard straggly, leggy plants and replace with vigorous cuttings.

PROPAGATION Divide the rhizome before starting into growth and ensure each section has a good bud. Or, take mid-summer cuttings, and raise in a peat/sand mix at 18°C/65°F.

SPECIES *K. digitaliflora* has pink flowers with green, spotted lobes. *K. amabilis (above)* has lighter pink flowers and pink spots. *K. bogotensis* has orange-red flowers with a yellow throat and red spots.

POSSIBLE PROBLEMS Generally trouble-free.

■ SPECIAL CARE TIP

The flowers are so attractive it's a shame to see the effect diminished by the occasional floppy stem. Support with a cane and tie in.

■ GARDENER'S TIP

Since K. amabilis *grows to 45cm/18in. It is ideal for a hanging basket and looks stunning surrounded with a cascading white and purple verbena.*

CLIANTHUS

| B/C | spring-summer | sun | 3m/10ft | 2.1m/7ft |

There are two species to chose from. The climbing *C. puniceus (above)*, with its beautiful four-fingered crimson flowers, and the prostrate *C. speciosus*. They are equally striking and unusual.

GROWING *C. p.*, known as lobster claw, is the easiest to grow. Plant in the border with its back to a trellis. Water freely over summer and ensure there is good ventilation, particularly on the hottest days. Prune back thoroughly in spring for a bushier specimen. *C. s.*, or glory pea, is ideal for a hanging basket but note it's unlikely to flower for more than one summer.

PROPAGATION Raise *C. p.* from seed in spring at a temperature of 16°C/61°F. It takes three years to get the plant to flower. *C. s.* also increases from seed. Be careful when potting up since its roots dislike being disturbed. Sow three per pot and thin out the weakest seedlings.

VARIETIES *C. p.* 'Albus' has similar claw-like flowers appearing in late spring and early summer. It climbs to 3m/10ft .

POSSIBLE PROBLEMS Red spider mite flock to the leaves.

GLORIOSA

| B/C | summer | sun | 1.8m/6ft | 60cm/24in |

The five-species genus of climbers is known as the glory lily. The flowers have six, upward-pointing fingers in orange, yellow/red, above glossy leaves.

GROWING Rest the tubers over winter at a minimum temperature of 13°C/55°F and pot up in early spring. Seven tubers will fit into a 25cm/10in pot filled with John Innes No 2; alternatively, use the greenhouse border and in both instances train up a trellis. An initial temperature of 16°C/61°F is required, with good humidity. In the growing season feed regularly and later, in autumn, as the foliage dies back, let the soil dry out.

PROPAGATION Remove offsets when the tubers are being repotted in spring. Raise at a temperature of 19°C/66°F.

SPECIES *G. rothschildiana (above)* has crimson and yellow flowers. *G. superba* has yellow-red flowers which fade to crimson and will succeed at slightly lower temperatures.

POSSIBLE PROBLEMS Generally trouble-free.

▦ SPECIAL CARE TIP

C. p. can be tried outdoors against a sheltered wall in a mild climate. Mulch its base over winter with a 30cm/12in deep layer of straw as frost protection.

▦ GARDENER'S TIP

Weave other climbers through a glory lilies' branches. The Chilean glory vine Eccremocarpus scaber (an annual) has complimentary red flowers.

HOYA

| B/C | summer | sun | 6m/20ft | 1.8m/6ft |

A tall evergreen climber whose size, and therefore flowering capacity, can be restricted by growing it in a medium-size pot. Given free growth it produces masses of waxy, white, star-like flowers each with a red centre. Highly scented nectar.

GROWING Use John Innes No 2 and train against a trellis up and under the greenhouse roof, like a vine. Good light and sun are essential, as is reasonable humidity. Spray twice daily. Let the soil dry a little between waterings, and keep much drier over winter. Severe temperature fluctuations lead to bud and leaf drop. Deadhead for a continuous flowering display.

PROPAGATION Increase by stem cuttings in early summer, each retaining three pairs of leaves.

SPECIES *H. bella* grows to 45cm/18in and is ideal for a hanging basket. *H. carnosa (above)* reaches 6m/20ft. If space is limited use a 15cm/6in pot; better still grow in a 30cm/12in pot; ideally raise in a bed. The scent is generally strongest in the evening.

POSSIBLE PROBLEMS Overwatering and lack of flower buds due to insufficient feeding.

LANTANA

| B/C | spring-autumn | sun | 90cm/36in | 90cm/36in |

An evergreen shrub from South America/West Indies which flowers from mid-spring virtually right through to mid-autumn. The species blooms in yellow and pink, but there are dozens of varieties in various shades of orange-red-yellow-pink, and white.

GROWING Young plants require John Innes No 2, the more mature No 3. Start off in a 20cm/8in pot in good sunlight, and provide good humidity on hot days. Established plants are cut back in late winter to within 7.5cm/3in of the base, with further pinching out for bushier specimens.

PROPAGATION In spring or autumn take 10cm/4in cuttings. A little bottom heat greatly assists in the formation of roots. Pinch out young plants.

SPECIES *L. camara (above)* is the taller, growing to 90cm/36in. The flowers turn from light to dark quite quickly giving extra colour shades. *L. montevidensis* is a good ground-cover plant reaching just 15cm/6in, and has light purple flowers.

POSSIBLE PROBLEMS Whitefly are a major hazard.

■ SPECIAL CARE TIP

H. bella *needs plenty of moisture to produce an abundance of honey-scented flowers. Place a wide tray of pebbles filled with water at the base of* the hanging basket and top up each day. It makes a significant difference.

■ WARNING

Though the flowers are harmless beware the foliage. It has a nasty smell, and produces unpleasant side effects should certain animals eat them.

AGAPETES

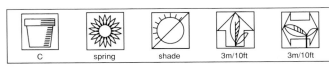

C	spring	shade	3m/10ft	3m/10ft

Highly unusual lantern-like flowers (usually red, white, yellow or pink) which dangle from the entire length of graceful pendulous branches. Well worth investigating.

GROWING The key to success is planting in a neutral/acid rich soil which provides good, quick drainage. Water well during the growing season, less vigorously at other times. Prune only to shape when the shrub is flopping messily, but otherwise leave well alone because the flowers only appear on ripe, mature wood. Tying-into canes is a better alternative.

PROPAGATION Toward the end of summer increase from youngish growth before it ripens.

SPECIES *A. serpens* is most widely available. The flowers are attractively patterned with dark markings. In a pot it should reach 1.8m/6ft. *A. rugosa* grows slightly taller and produces clusters of white flowers with purple markings. *A. macrantha (above)* has narrow pinkish-white flowers.

POSSIBLE PROBLEMS Generally trouble-free.

CYMBIDIUM

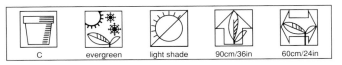

C	evergreen	light shade	90cm/36in	60cm/24in

Cymbidium are graceful, evergreen, epiphytic orchids. Most of them originate from the Far East and Australia.

GROWING If growing in a pot use special orchid compost consisting of bark, loam, and spagnum moss. Plant in a 12.5cm/5in container with plenty of drainage material and pot up in alternate years. Cymbidium can reach a huge size needing 50cm/20in containers. Provide continuous humidity, never letting the atmosphere dry out.

PROPAGATION Increase by division in spring. Each section should have roots and top growth. Water in after one week.

SPECIES *C. Pontac* 'Mont Millais' flowers in spring with layers of dark red and white petals; *C. devonianum* has green and purple flowers, and blooms in summer. *C. grandiflorum* has brown spots and green flowers, and blooms in winter.

POSSIBLE PROBLEMS Scale insects; aphids; red spider mite; leaf discolouration.

■ GARDENER'S TIP

The most exciting variety is the hybrid 'Ludgvan Cross'. It has red-pink lantern flowers edged lime green, with dark veining. It is a cross between A. s. and A. incurvata. *If you see one for sale buy it there and then because they are not often available.*

■ GARDENER'S TIP

The trickiest side to growing orchids is knowing when to water. The barkheavy compost always seems dry. If the pot feels extremely light, give the orchid a drink. If the plants are to flower over winter, ensure that they have a light-shady, airy position throughout the summer.

EUPHORBIA

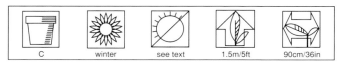

C	winter	see text	1.5m/5ft	90cm/36in

The most popular greenhouse euphorbia is *E. pulcherrima (above)* or the poinsettia, a brash and tricky plant. It has striking red bracts but won't easily repeat this showy performance a second year.

GROWING Keep at approximately 18°C/65°F. When the bracts have died down cut back the plant almost to the base, and reduce watering so the soil is virtually dry. In early summer kick-start it into life with fresh compost and water. Feed regularly and for the next two months provide a minimum of 14-hours darkness per day. When the new bracts start to colour you can put an end to this regime. Those successful in keeping a poinsettia going should note that it will get bigger year by year and could reach a maximum height of approximately 1.5m/5ft.

PROPAGATION After pruning, use new shoots as cuttings.

SPECIES There are 2000 species of euphorbia. *E. fulgens* is one of the most similar to poinsettia and has smaller scarlet bracts.

POSSIBLE PROBLEMS The main danger is not giving the correct number of hours of darkness. This is absolutely crucial.

CYCLAMEN

C	spring	semi-shade	20cm/8in	20cm/8in

C. persicum (above) is the plant for the greenhouse. It has a light scent – lily-of-the-valley to some, intoxicating, stale cardboard to others – and flowers like Flemish hats. Each has five, white, vertical twisted petals, with a crimson ring at the base. The foliage has ornate mottling of dark and pale green. The florist's cyclamen is scentless but has larger flowers.

GROWING Plant *C. p.*'s corm in a 15cm/6in pot filled with John Innes No 1 and plenty of drainage material. Give good ventilation over summer (eg a cold frame) and little watering. Cease altogether in mid-summer when there's no new foliage. In late summer pot up, with the top edge of the corm just visible above the soil. Commence watering and bring under glass in autumn, maintaining a temperature of at least 10°C/50°F.

PROPAGATION Since the corms will not divide, increase by seeds sown in winter at 16°C/61°F. Water sensibly because too little or too much can be fatal. Pot up into 6cm/2½in pots.

VARIETIES *C. p.* 'Silberstrahl'; *C. p.* 'Rex' has green and bright white mottled leaves.

POSSIBLE PROBLEMS Vine weevil; botrytis.

▨ SPECIAL CARE TIP

Poinsettias bleed a rather irritating sap, so when cutting back make always sure you are wearing a pair of gardening gloves.

▨ GARDENER'S TIP

Most books recommend throwing away the corms after flowering, but if treated properly they live to a ripe age and flower abundantly year after year.

AZALEA

| C | early spring | light shade | 30cm/12in | 30cm/12in |

Greenhouse azaleas are far trickier to grow than outdoor kinds, but they give a sensational flowering display. Excellent as late winter gifts.

GROWING Provide a steady temperature of 16°C/61°F, with moist, shady conditions. After flowering, deadhead and spray against botrytis. In mid-spring pot up using only lime-free compost otherwise you'll kill the plant, and give the occasional liquid feed. Only use rain or cold, boiled water. Increase ventilation, and from early summer to mid-autumn plunge the pot outside in a sheltered shady bed so its rim is level with the ground. Keep the soil moist. Return the pot to the greenhouse in autumn and wait for the next crop of flower buds.

PROPAGATION This is a job for the professionals. You can try grafting or taking cuttings but it is a slow, precise science and generally not worth attempting.

SPECIES The choice is limited but the many varieties of *Rhododendron simsii* (Indian azalea; *above*) are very suitable for growing in the greenhouse.

POSSIBLE PROBLEMS Watch out for aphids, they can be quite a nuisance.

BRUNFELSIA

| B/C | summer | light shade | 1m/3ft 3in | 45cm/18in |

B. americana, lady of the night, is a stunning little plant with good fragrance. *B. calycina macrantha*, yesterday, today, and tomorrow, is known for its rapid turnover of flowers. They unfold in purple-blue and fade to white in just three days.

GROWING Raise in a 15cm/6in pot filled with John Innes No 2. Over the winter water sparingly but increase during the growing period. Although the plants will tolerate temperatures as low as 5°C/40°F in mid-winter, they really need 18°C/65°F for a long, vigorous, flowering season. During the summer provide good ventilation and protection from direct, scorching sunlight. Fresh soil each spring and a weak liquid feed every fortnight is all that's required.

PROPAGATION Increase by cuttings of soft growth, approximately 5cm/2in long. Insert into a peat compost with plenty of sand and raise at 21°C/70°F.

VARIETIES *B. pauciflora (above)* is easily raised and has faintly scented flowers set against a rich green foliage. *B. undulata* and *B. americana*, both from the West Indies, have white-cream flowers with stronger scent.

POSSIBLE PROBLEMS Generally trouble-free.

ORGANIC TIP

To keep the soil moist over summer mulch with pine needles – either spruce or conifer. Shredded or pulverized bark is another possibility.

COLLECTOR'S TIP

It's well worth growing one of the West Indian plants in the greenhouse border, given there's adequate room. The small shrubs can easily reach 1.2m/4ft, possibly even higher, given a free root-run, and they give off extra, pervasive scent.

COLEUS

| C | evergreen | light shade | 45cm/18in | 30cm/12in |

Coleus are evergreen perennial plants from Africa and the Far East. They're grown for their bright, showy, patterned foliage and can either stand alone or be the foreground to larger, flowering plants.

GROWING Keep slightly shaded at first, though older plants will tolerate direct sun provided they are well-watered. The plant will quickly wilt without regular waterings. Feed often for good leaf colour and remove any flowers the moment they start to swell or the leaf colour will fade.

PROPAGATION Grow from seeds in spring. Seeds are available in a good range of mixtures and as individual, named varieties. In addition they can be grown from cuttings which root easily at any time during late spring and summer. Pot the seedlings into 9cm/3½in pots.

SPECIES *C. blumei* has reddish central leaves edged lime green/yellow. *C. thrysoideus* produces bright blue, tubular flowers from late autumn to early spring.

POSSIBLE PROBLEMS Whitefly; mealy bug.

CALADIUM

| C | evergreen | light shade | 38cm/15in | 30cm/12in |

Caladium are greenhouse tuberous perennials which unfold spectacular, brightly patterned leaves. *C. × hortulanum*, angel's wings, is top of the range with creamy-white centres, mottled green edging, and crimson veining.

GROWING Start the tubers into growth in early spring at 21°C/70°F. Place in a box of moist peat and, when growth begins, pot into a small container filled with John Innes No 2. Provide a thick layer of drainage material at the bottom. When the leaves begin to appear water freely and increase the humidity. In mid-summer give a regular liquid feed. Decrease both feed and water as the foliage fades in the autumn, and store the tuber in a frost-free room at approximately 13°C/55°F, gently wetting the soil occasionally.

PROPAGATION In spring carefully remove new offsets from the parent tuber. Pot up singly as described above.

VARIETIES *C. bicolor (above)*: 'Pink Cloud' has pink mottling in the leaf centre with whitish veins. 'Pink Beauty' has similar pink mottling but with pink-purple veins; and 'John Peed' has bright rusty centres and crimson veining.

POSSIBLE PROBLEMS Generally trouble-free.

◼ GARDENER'S TIP

Unlike other coleus C. b verschaffeltii should keep some of its flowers. They are a delightful blue and stand out against the contrasting red foliage.

◼ SPECIAL CARE TIP

Caladium are such a good talking point it's a shame not to bring them into the house. You can do this over summer, but don't rush the process. First, gradually acclimatize the plant to the lower humidity and temperature. Treat it sensitively and it won't react badly.

GYNURA

| B/C | spring | sun | 1.2m/4ft | 50cm/20in |

Gynura, or the velvet nettle, is a semi-climbing plant with fleshy foliage and a violet sheen.

GROWING Give the gynura a well-lit position which helps to bring out the leaf colour, as does pinching out the orange-yellow dandelion-like flowers. In summer shade from direct, fierce sunlight and grow in 13cm/5in pots filled with John Innes No 2. To avoid overwatering allow the compost to become slightly dry before the next application. In winter provide a minimum temperature of 10°C/50°F.

PROPAGATION In spring take a 7.5cm/3in long stem and dip in rooting powder. Insert into a 9cm/3½in pot of sand and peat. When rooted repot with John Innes No 1.

SPECIES *G. aurantiaca*, the velvet plant, has violet hairy stems and flowers in spring; height 3m/10ft. *G. sarmentosa* *(above)* has purple-green leaves and is smaller at 1.2m/4ft.

POSSIBLE PROBLEMS Generally trouble-free.

KALANCHOE

| C | late winter/spring | sun | 25cm/10in | 25cm/10in |

Perennial fleshy succulents grown for their foliage and prolific flower clusters. The Madagascan *Kalanchoe blossfeldiana* in particular has produced excellent hybrids with red, orange, and yellow blooms.

GROWING Use 20cm/8in pots filled with John Innes No 2 and keep at 10°C/50°F over winter in good sunlight. Water moderately allowing the soil to become dryish between applications.

PROPAGATION At any time from late spring to mid-summer take 10cm/4in cuttings and raise in John Innes No 1.

SPECIES You'll need to wait for *K. beharensis* to become a substantial 2m/6ft 6in before it flowers (yellow). At half the height, *K. daigremontiana* has more attractive, vertical, dark green leaves with notched edges. The flowers are pink. The panda plant, *K. tomentosa*, is similarly shaped with leaves covered in furry hair. It produces yellow flowers. *K. tubiflora* is the most intriguing; it has a single stem bearing dozens of orange bells in early spring. *K. pumila (above)* makes an excellent hanging basket.

POSSIBLE PROBLEMS Mealy bug.

◼ GARDENER'S TIP

G. s. also doubles as an excellent trailing plant. Group four into a 30cm/12in hanging basket and prune to avoid any excess straggliness.

◼ PROPAGATING TIP

Instead of taking stem cuttings, try sowing seed. Germinate them at a temperature of 23°C/73°F in John Innes No 1, and thin out to the strongest.

GLOXINIA

| C | spring-summer | light shade | 60cm/24in | 30cm/12in |

Gloxinia are popular, tender perennials grown from tubers. They produce bright, trumpet-like flowers in a wide range of colours. Strictly speaking, they should be listed as *Sinningia speciosa*.

GROWING Start the tubers into growth in spring. Lay them on moist compost, the side with the slight hollow in the middle being on top. When shoots start to appear, pot each one individually in a 13cm/5in pot with the top of the tuber just visible above the compost (John Innes No 2). Water sparingly at the start, and gradually increase, with a liquid feed. Keep in light shade and reduce watering when the foliage turns yellow. Over winter store the tubers in a dry place at a minimum of 10°C/50°F.

PROPAGATION Divide the tuber in spring, ensuring each section has a good shoot.

SPECIES *G. perennis* has pale blue flowers; height 50cm/20in.

POSSIBLE PROBLEMS Generally trouble-free.

PERISTROPHE

| C | winter | sun | 90cm/36in | 60cm/24in |

Exotic, bright, Christmas-flowering plants which need high summer temperatures to thrive. They could also be grown in the tropical greenhouse.

GROWING Pinch out young plants to increase bushiness and flower potential. Grow in John Innes No 3 and give a regular feed over the growing season when the temperature should be at least 18°C/65°F. Good ventilation is also required. In the spring cut back to encourage new growth.

PROPAGATION In spring take 10cm/4in stem cuttings of the new growth and raise in a peat and sand mix at 18°C/65°F.

SPECIES *P. hyssopifolia* has cherry-red flowers. *P. h.* 'Auto-variegata' has marvellous green, white, yellowish foliage and scarlet flowers and *P. speciosa (above)* has mauve-purple flowers that stand out against the dark green foliage.

POSSIBLE PROBLEMS Generally trouble-free.

■ PROPAGATING TIP

Gloxinia can also be raised from seed. A spring sowing and constant 24-hour temperature of 18°C/65°F will give flowering plants in just six months.

■ GARDENER'S TIP

For an instant, bright, bold, three-plant Christmas present try a purple peristrophe, a poinsettia, and a white cyclamen with mottled foliage.

TIBOUCHINA

| B/C | summer | sun | 3.6m/12ft | 1.8m/6ft |

An absolute 'must'. *T. urvilleana (above)*, the Brazilian spider plant, is a mini, stately shrub with felt-like leaves and large, bright, violet flowers. In a big pot and a tall greenhouse it becomes a 3.6m/12ft tree. Far more easily raised than its exotic appearance suggests.

GROWING Young plants are given John Innes No 2 and a light position. Support the central stem with a cane. Also, keep turning the pot or the initially flimsy horizontal stems will all bend significantly towards the light. Water infrequently over winter, increasingly in summer when a weekly feed is required. The higher the temperature the sooner the summer flowering begins. In spring cut back to induce extra growth and to avoid straggliness. Note some new growth has an initial protective sheath.

PROPAGATION Use prunings, 10cm/4in long, and pot up in a peat and sand mix. Raise at a temperature of 18°C/65°F.

VARIETIES 'Grandiflora' has even larger flowers than *T. u.*.

POSSIBLE PROBLEMS Caterpillars feast on the lush foliage.

STREPTOCARPUS

| C | spring-autumn | sun | 45cm/18in | 45cm/18in |

Unless you rest the easily grown Cape primrose it's quite capable of flowering for nearly 12 months, exhausting itself and eventually dying. The flowers are carried singly or in clusters of three or four at the end of slender stems 30cm/12in long. They are coloured in shades of blue, violet, white, pink and magenta.

GROWING Increase watering in the spring and shade from fierce, burning sunlight. If the greenhouse temperature exceeds 18°C/65°F, ventilate. The Cape primrose grows fast and needs a fortnightly feed and constant humidity. Remove the first, early flush of flower buds at the start of summer to build up the plant's strength for a more concentrated flower display later on. Rest over winter.

PROPAGATION In early winter divide established crowns and pot up in a sand and peat mix at a temperature of 18°C/65°F. With growth transfer to 10cm/3in pots.

SPECIES *S. dunnii* (with rose coloured flowers), *S. galpinii* (mauve and white), and *S. parviflorus* come from South Africa. Save for the latter they produce one immense leaf with a large stem carrying many flowers.

POSSIBLE PROBLEMS Aphids feed on the tender young growth.

■ SPECIAL CARE TIP

If the plant hasn't grown too big and heavy, move it outdoors in summer. The only drawback is that a heavy downpour can smash the flowers.

■ PROPAGATING TIP

Streptocarpus are also easily raised from seed. Germinate at 18°C/65°F in John Innes No 1 under a fine, sieved layer of compost. The mid-winter

grown plants will flower eight months later, while seeds sown in spring will not flower for approximately 14 months.

TROPICAL EXOTICA

18° CENTIGRADE / 65° FAHRENHEIT

You would think that the higher the minimum winter temperature, the more the ultimate hothouse would contain jazzy outbreaks of colour. To a certain extent this is true. However, as is evident from the following plant selection, foliage and spathes start to come into their own, and on many occasions they easily out-perform the flowers.

SURPRISE FEATS *Anthurium andreanum* is justifiably called the painter's palette. This Colombian plant, which grows to a modest 45cm/18in, produces 70 sq cm/1 sq ft of shiny spathe from late spring to the end of summer. From certain angles it looks just like a brash, plastic pair of 'kiss-me-quick' lips. Other

species, notably *A. wendlandii*, are capable of even more lurid growth but are often too big for the domestic greenhouse.

Monstera deliciosa is a giant. Its mellow, yellow spathe has won the name Swiss cheese plant though it looks more like a cocoon for corn on the cob. In the wild the plant literally hauls itself up through the vegetation to heights of 5m/15ft by means of vigorous aerial roots. They wrap themselves around trees, like the end of a whip, hunting out extra nourishment. If it shows similar colonising tendencies in your green-house you've obviously discovered the right way to raise it, though you may need to curb its greedy habits by snipping back the more active roots.

Aglaonema pictum is much more coy about its spathe, and is the best choice for a less theatrical hothouse. Above the dark and grey-green mottled foliage, 15cm/6in long, appears a cylindrical, hand-size, yellow curve. It's exciting nonetheless.

The foliage performers are rather different. The magnified leaves of caladium might be modern art. The edges are green, the centre creamy-white, and the principal markings a criss-cross of crimson lines. They are far more delightful than the flowers of many a highly respected plant, yet irritatingly the growing conditions are quite demanding. They require the atmospheric equivalent of a hot-and-wet South American rain forest.

LUXURY SHRUBS There's nothing more infuriating than buying an expensive gardenia running wild with swollen flower buds, getting it home, and in a different atmosphere watching them drop, unopened, intolerant, selfishly refusing to show their porcelain petals and refusing to emit the highest quality fragrance.

Gardenia need high temperatures almost as much as high humidity, and provided you master the right growing conditions and remember its dislike of lime,

a small plant can leap into a 1.5m/5ft shrub. The foliage has its own glossy attractions. Two varieties – 'Florida' and 'Fortuniana' – flower in summer while 'Veitchiana' opens its buds in winter.

The non-scented hibiscus is a shrub of about the same size and makes a fine companion plant. It has a rapid turnover of trumpet-like flowers available in shades of red, pink, yellow, and cream; the current list of varieties, beside those mentioned *on page 87*, includes 'Casablanca', 'Helene', and 'Holiday'.

RARITY VALUE Gardenia and hibiscus may be sensational, but neither could possibly be described as rare. *Polianthes* is a better candidate, though only because it's sometimes prone to virus attack which ruins and discolours the foliage. If you can beat that problem it results in some of the most exotically beautiful flowers. Each is approximately 2.5cm/1in long, white, and has such a powerful scent that some gardeners actually find it quite overpowering. It's worth growing if only to see what they mean.

The mimosa in total contrast is a retiring specimen. Just as a hedgehog dislikes being touched, and rolls up when prodded, so in its way does *Mimosa pudica*. The

Humidifiers in a tropical greenhouse throw out fine mists of water to maintain constant humidity, in order to mirror the plants native habitat.

plant is covered in thousands of tiny hinges, or pulvini, situated at the base of the leaves and leaflets. Touch the foliage and it literally shuts up. The only problem is that it's really an annual, for while you can cut back to produce new growth, the prompt, reactions increasingly diminish with the seasons.

HOTHOUSE CARE As with all types of greenhouse it's absolutely crucial to keep the very warmest free of pests and diseases. The better the conditions for the plants, the better they are for unwanted guests, and the more vigilant you have got to be.

Slacken up and a first-rate collection of plants that perform in very different, stylish ways, might end up being carted off to the bonfire. If you can perform to your best, rather like a stage manager, and keep the environment clean and above all humid, the plants need little encouragement to do their bit. And tropical exotica at their best take an awful lot of beating.

GARDENIA

| C | summer | light shade | 90cm/36in | 90cm/36in |

An exotic plant with a sensational scent. Since it is usually quite expensive don't buy unless you can guarantee providing ideal conditions. It is quite fussy and doesn't adapt well.

GROWING Use John Innes No 2 and over the winter keep at a temperature of 15°C/60°F. Shade from strong sunshine and give ventilation carefully to avoid cold draughts and a fall in temperature. Good humidity is essential. In summer increase the temperature to 21°C/70°F and water liberally using rain or cold, boiled water. Feed regularly.

PROPAGATION Take cuttings of young wood and insert into a mix of peat and sand. Raise at a minimum temperature of 21°C/70°F.

SPECIES *G. jasminoides (above)*, Cape jasmine, is the most commonly available kind.

POSSIBLE PROBLEMS Mealy bug, particularly on neglected plants.

POLIANTHES

| C | summer | sun | 1m/3ft 3in | 30cm/12in |

P. tuberosa (above) is a far too rarely grown, powerfully scented, Mexican perennial with beautiful cream-white flowers. It needs careful handling.

GROWING In the autumn plant singly in a pot filled with John Innes No 1 and good drainage material. The winter temperature can sink to 13°C/55°F but should increase to 18°C/65°F in spring. Only water after growth appears and keep in the light. Over winter store in a tray of sand.

PROPAGATION Detach offsets in the autumn. Unless they have benefited from constant high temperatures they are unlikely to flower.

VARIETIES *P. t.* 'Pearl' has an even richer scent. Since some people find this too overpowering, it's worth comparing it with *P. t.* to see which you prefer.

POSSIBLE PROBLEMS Sometimes prone to virus attack.

▨ GARDENER'S TIP

If you are addicted to heady scents but cannot provide gardenia with constant, demanding, high humidity, jasmine is the best alternative. Not only is it easy to bring into flower year after year, but you can bring pots indoors in late winter. In spring the scent wafts through the rooms.

▨ GARDENER'S TIP

It's very easy to get addicted to the strong, heady fragrance. Plant a whole succession of the tubers and bring them into growth one after another, say at three-week intervals. As the flowers gradually open and release their fragrance so they can be brought indoors.

CLERODENDRUM

| B/C | summer | semi-shade | 3m/10ft | 1.8m/6ft |

Some species are hardy flowering shrubs, others, such as *C. thomsoniae (above)*, are exotic hothouse climbers. For the showiest flowering display, let them grow unchecked.

GROWING Start newly potted plants into growth at 18°C/65°F. Since root development is quite vigorous the greenhouse border is better than a pot, though if using the latter begin with a 25cm/10in container filled with John Innes No 2. Spray regularly and tie-in new shoots to a trellis. After flowering prune back all growth with blossom to within 7.5m/3in of the base. Water liberally during the growing season and keep on the dry side over winter. Feed established plants with a weak fertilizer.

PROPAGATION The quickest method involves taking 10cm/4in long pieces of stem in spring and rooting them in a sand and peat compost. Raise at a temperature of 21°C/70°F.

SPECIES *C. t.* has a white calyx with a red corolla and can easily reach 3m/10ft. *C. splendens* grows to the same height and also produces an abundance of flowers, except they are scarlet. Rather shrubbier, and for those who cannot guarantee continuous high temperatures, is the scented *C. fragrans pleniflorum* which survives at a minimum winter temperature of 10°C/50°F.

POSSIBLE PROBLEMS Generally trouble-free.

AGLAONEMA

| C | summer | shade | 60cm/24in | 60cm/24in |

In the wild it grows on forest floors where the conditions are dark, damp and humid. It compensates for a lack of flowers with marbled green and white swathes of foliage. Looks good when placed among other exotic plants.

GROWING Enjoys peat-based John Innes No 3, possibly used 50-50 with John Innes No 2. *A. versicolor* is trickier to grow than the other varieties, and is really too fussy to bother with.

PROPAGATION Take shoot tip cuttings in late spring. Each should be attached to a number of leaves and rooted at 21°C/70°F. Although you can increase by seed at the same time of year, you need higher temperatures (27°C/81°F) and even then good results cannot be guaranteed.

SPECIES Three of the most attractive varieties, which are also easily grown, are *A. commutatum* 'Treubii' with creamy patterning, *A. crispum* 'Silver Queen' (with distinguished pale green leaves flecked with silver), and *A. pictum* with greyish patches.

POSSIBLE PROBLEMS Mealy bug.

■ COLLECTOR'S TIP

Non-greenhouse climbing clerodenrum are definitely frost-tender and need to be planted in the most sheltered part of a mild-climate garden. C. bungeri (from China), with clusters of pink, slightly fragrant flowers, is a good choice. It grows to 2.1m/7ft high by 2.1m/7ft.

■ GARDENER'S TIP

Lovers of epiphytic plants, which grow and root on branches, often struggle to find good, exotic companion plants. In this case the best are probably in their own genus. Group together three or four species, with their mottled, lush, upright leaves and striking spathes. A first-rate choice.

DIEFFENBACHIA

| C | evergreen | light shade | 1.2m/4ft | 1.2m/4ft |

Don't be fooled by the glossy, attractive foliage. Swallow the poisonous sap and you'll find it difficult to talk, hence the common names dumb cane, and the ironic mother-in-law. Nonetheless this is definitely worth growing and quite safe to handle.

GROWING Though dieffenbachia can be grown as a houseplant it succeeds best in greenhouses. Provide humidity for good leaf colour; water liberally over summer and sparingly in winter. If the leaves start to yellow increase the temperature.

PROPAGATION Detach suckers growing at the base and plant up in a mix of sand and peat. Alternatively, if the plant is getting too straggly, cut back and use 10cm/4in lengths of stem tip. These can also be grown by laying them in a tray of peat and sand at a temperature of 24°C/75°F. When they have developed a root system pot up in a 7.5cm/3in container.

SPECIES *D. maculata* and *D. m.* 'Exotica' have green and white, exuberantly mottled leaves. *D. picta* has similar patterning in lime green. *D. amoena (above)* has large, oblong shaped leaves.

POSSIBLE PROBLEMS Stem rotting if overwatered.

CODIAEUM

| C | summer | sun | 1.2m/4ft | 90cm/36in |

One of the few plants which needs to have its flowers automatically removed. They are not that attractive, and detract from the large, heavily veined, leathery, multicoloured leaves splashed in yellow-green-orange-red.

GROWING For the richest leaf colour give ample light, humid conditions and, crucially, steady temperatures. Fluctuations quickly lead to leaf drop. Also wipe the leaves to emphasize their glossiness. Start off young plants in 8cm/3in pots and move up to size 15cm/6in.

PROPAGATION The plants inevitably grow tall and leggy. When this happens cut back to encourage new growth lower down. The pruned tip sections (7.5cm/3in) can be used as cuttings. Cut off only the very bottom leaves so there will be foliage from the soil upward.

VARIETIES *C. variegatum* and *C. v. pictum (above)* both grow to 45cm/18in and have a wide range of colours.

POSSIBLE PROBLEMS Red spider mite; mealy bugs.

■ GARDENER'S TIP

The striking foliage is best offset by growing the plant near a tibouchiana, or any other plant well-covered in large purple flowers.

■ GARDENER'S TIP

Codiaeum look so good that they deserve to be brought indoors. Make sure they'll be at the same temperature and always keep out of draughts.

FITTONIA

C	evergreen	light shade	17cm/7in	40cm/16in

Trailing plants with rich, ornamental foliage. *F. verschaffeltii* *(above)* has red-veined green foliage; *F. v.* 'Argyroneura' has slightly smaller leaves (10cm/4in) with white lines.

GROWING Provide a shaded position and good humidity. Don't let the winter temperature drop below 16°C/61°F and keep the compost dry in the dormant season. The plants generally decline rapidly with age and after a couple of seasons should be replaced by new specimens. They also tend to spread and scramble all over the place, in which case prune back to the new growth to maintain shape.

PROPAGATION Increase by removing offsets in late spring. Alternatively, divide the plant and retain fresh, vigorous growth while removing the tired centre.

SPECIES *F. gigantea* sometimes produces insignificant yellow flowers. *F. v.* 'Nana' is the small, compact version of *F. v.* 'Argyroneura'.

POSSIBLE PROBLEMS Generally trouble-free.

HAEMANTHUS

C	summer	sun	30cm/12in	15cm/6in

The blood lily is a rarely grown tender bulb from South Africa with unusual, striking flowers. Only half a dozen species are generally available, and even then some are listed as scadoxus.

GROWING Raise in 20cm/8in pots filled with John Innes No 2 at 18°C/65°F. Insert the bulbs up to the tip and water in. Feed over summer and keep moist through the winter.

PROPAGATION Increase by offsets in the spring. Pot up and keep the roots packed into a small space. Add horticultural sand for quick drainage.

SPECIES *H. albiflos* has a striking mass of white flowers. *H. coccineus* has scarlet cupped flowers on short, stout stems. The yellow stamens resemble the tip of a thick brush and after fading are followed by dramatic leaves. *H. katherinae*'s *(above)* bloom is actually a ball of star-shaped red flowers, followed by red fruit.

POSSIBLE PROBLEMS Mealy bugs.

■ SPECIAL CARE TIP

Because of fittonia's attractive reddish leaf it is tempting to bring one indoors and position against a white wall for colour contrast. Avoid the temptation though. Fittonias do not, under any circumstances, like a dry atmosphere. They are definitely suited to the more humid tropical greenhouse.

■ SPECIAL CARE TIP

Haemanthus doesn't like being disturbed. Leave in the pot and only remove every third year. Scrape away top soil and replace in the spring.

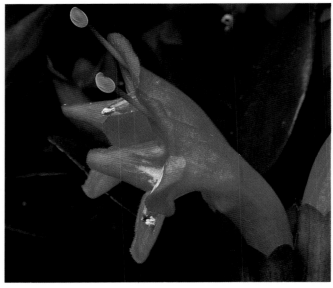

ANTHURIUM

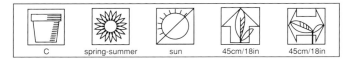

C	spring-summer	sun	45cm/18in	45cm/18in

Just about the most striking plant around with its blowsy flowering spathes, and glossy foliage.

GROWING Use a free-draining peaty soil with plenty of sphagnum moss and a handful of charcoal, and keep at a constant high temperature around 18°C/65°F. Water sparingly over winter but much more freely over the growing period. Splash water around the pot to keep the atmosphere humid, and spray the leaves during a hot spell. As the stems elongate they should be wrapped with moss to encourage root formation.

PROPAGATION The easiest method involves removing the plant from its pot in spring and dividing in two. Ensure both halves have a good root system.

SPECIES *A. andreanum (above)* has an exotic waxy spathe in red, white or pink. Rather more baroque is *A. scherzerianum* with its spadix spiralling out of the red spathe. Probably the grandest anthurium of all is *A. wendlandii* which grows to a gross 2.1/7ft mound with blue-grey spadix, giving a decent flower display and red fruit. Otherwise, species are the size of the typical pot plant and far more manageable.

POSSIBLE PROBLEMS Aphids; leaf spot.

AESCHYNANTHUS

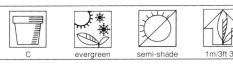

C	evergreen	semi-shade	1m/3ft 3in	60cm/24in

Evergreen trailing perennials from the Far East and Malaysia with exotic flowers. Though they can easily withstand winter temperatures of 7°C/45°F, they need higher temperatures of around 18°C/65°F to thrive.

GROWING Aeschynanthus is ideal for planting in a pot or hanging basket. The lower its winter temperature the less it needs to be watered. It reacts extremely badly to cold winter draughts which make it shed its leaves. Feed regularly over the growing season and spray the surrounding air when very hot. Cut back every third spring to encourage new growth, and repot.

PROPAGATION In late spring create new plants from non-flowering shoot tips, 5cm/2in long. Keep at a slightly higher temperature than the parent plant.

SPECIES *A. lobbianus (above)* has thick, shiny green leaves and batches of purple-red flowers throughout the summer. *A. pulcher* offers tubular red flowers with the additional advantage of yellow throats, and flowers over a slightly longer period, until early autumn.

POSSIBLE PROBLEMS Generally trouble-free.

▪ GARDENER'S TIP

Since anthurium are epiphytic grow them on artificial branches. Wrap around with sphagnum moss and tie in the root system.

▪ SPECIAL CARE TIP

Be careful not to get water splashes on the leaves when spraying the plant. Under a fierce sun this leads to ugly marks which are difficult to eradicate.

HIBISCUS

| C | summer | sun | 1.8m/6ft | 1.5m/5ft |

The Chinese rose, *H. rosa-sinensis (above)*, and particularly *H. r-s.* 'Cooperi', are the most suitable for the greenhouse. They have large, crimson, trumpet-like flowers, and without the root restrictions of a pot will quickly turn into a large shrub.

GROWING Hibiscus will eventually need a 30cm/12in pot filled with John Innes No 3. Keep a steady summer temperature of 18°C/65°F; any deviation leads to bud drop. Over winter provide a temperature of 16°C/61°F to avoid leaf drop. Prune in spring both to keep size under control and to prevent the base becoming bare and leggy. Good ventilation is necessary on the hottest summer days. Repot each spring.

PROPAGATION Take 10cm/4in heel cuttings in spring and raise in a sand and peat mix at 18°C/65°F. After rooting, pot up in John Innes No 2.

SPECIES *H. r-s.* 'Cooperi' has the more attractive foliage with green, creamy-white and red leaves. It is also better suited to smaller greenhouses since it can be grown in 15cm/6in pots.

POSSIBLE PROBLEMS Aphids; mealy bugs; red spider mite.

CANNA

| B/C | summer | sun | 1.2m/4ft | 90cm/36in |

Famous for its exotic flowers and ornamental foliage. The most popular forms are *C. indica* hybrids, like 'The President', which comes in a flashy range of pink, red, orange and yellow.

GROWING Porous, rich potting compost is ideal (John Innes No 3) above a deep layer of drainage material. Start the tubers into growth in late winter at a temperature of 15°C/60°F and increase to 18°C/65°F. A single crown needs a 15cm/6in pot, larger clumps require 20cm/8in containers. When growth is under way place in full sunlight and give a weekly feed throughout the summer. When growth dies down cease watering and dry off the tuber.

PROPAGATION Just before or while the tuber puts on spring growth, lift and divide. Each portion must have one or more crowns with a few roots.

SPECIES *C. iridiflora*, from Peru, grows a little taller and is better suited to the greenhouse border. Its swarm of orange petals look like butterflies. It can be grown outdoors in mild climates. The hybrid 'Lucifer' *(above)* grows to a height of 1m/3ft 3in.

POSSIBLE PROBLEMS Beware of snails which feed on the unfurled foliage in spring.

▪ COLLECTOR'S TIP

H. schizopetalus *is much more of a climbing rambler, it can easily stretch to 3m/10ft high and 1.2m/4ft wide. Give it complete freedom by growing it in* *the greenhouse border and train other colourful climbers in and out of its branches.*

▪ PROPATING TIP

Canna can be propagated by seed but they are quite difficult to germinate. Soak the small, tough nuts overnight in a tray of water and then plant up at 26°C/80°F. *The only problem with this method is that the flowers rarely appear before the third year.*

MONSTERA

| B/C | evergreen | light shade | 2.1m/7ft | 2.1m/7ft |

The Mexican Swiss cheese plant makes a monstrous growth of glossy, indented foliage among a swirl of aerial roots grabbing at nearby vegetation for extra moisture. Impressive, and definitely not one for the smaller greenhouse.

GROWING Use John Innes No 3 and keep the soil moist over the growing season, dryish over winter. To prevent the aerial roots attacking other plants wrap together the former in wet moss. Particularly vigorous roots can be snipped off. Specimens grown in large pots (30cm/12in) or borders will need tying-in to stout stakes for support. High humidity is essential for abundant growth, good indentation, and the dramatic, pale orange flowering spathe (like corn-on-the cob) which only appears on established plants.

PROPAGATION Increase by side shoots which are teased away from the parent when they are 5cm/2in long. Pot up in a 13cm/5in pot filled with John Innes No 3.

SPECIES *M. deliciosa (above)* is the one for the greenhouse.

POSSIBLE PROBLEMS Generally trouble-free.

PHILODENDRON

| B/C | evergreen | semi-shade | 1.8m/6ft | 1.8m/6ft |

Though these tall South American evergreens can easily be grown as houseplants, they need a tropical greenhouse to produce their best foliage. The leaves tend to be either spear-like and 20cm/8in long, or incised and 60cm/24in long.

GROWING Humidity and a trellis clad in damp moss are the two keys for success. Increase pot size to a maximum of 30cm/12in and water sparingly over winter. Tie in new growth to the support and keep the moss wet for the aerial roots. Give a summer feed and rest over winter.

PROPAGATION Take a 12.5cm/5in stem cutting in early summer with one leaf. Raise at 26°C/80°F in John Innes No 1 and within three seasons it should reach 1m/3ft 3in.

SPECIES *P. scandens (above)* is a rampant climber, with heart-shape leaves and grows to a height 1.8m/6ft. Grow inshade. *P. melanochryson*, from Colombia, has velvety, olive-green foliage and is the same height. Two non-climbers are *P. bipinnatifidum* (1.2m/4ft), which resembles the Swiss cheese plant, and *P. selloum*, (1m/3ft 3in).

POSSIBLE PROBLEMS Generally trouble-free.

■ SPECIAL CARE TIP

Though they can be grown as houseplants, and be restricted in size, their leaves tend to lose their perforations in the typical dry household atmosphere.

Regular sprayings are therefore essential, as are canes well-wrapped with wet sphagnum moss.

■ COLLECTOR'S TIP

P. erubescens 'Burgundy' *is justifiably referred to as blushing philodendron. The new foliage has a flame-copper tinge which produces a theatrical*

contrast with the older, dark green leaves. Extra pinching out is essential in order to gain the full, dramatic effect.

TILLANDSIA

| C | summer | light shade | 30cm/12in | 30cm/12in |

A wide-ranging group of bromeliads, some of which are epiphytes. They range from pin-cushion like growths to Spanish moss which engulfs trees in humid, hot conditions.

GROWING Pot-grown species such as *T. cyanea (above)* and *T. linenii* need a leafmould compost with plenty of horticultural sand. Water infrequently out of season with rain or cold, boiled water, increasingly over summer. The humidity must be high so spray at least three times a day to prevent the atmosphere from drying out.

PROPAGATION In late spring carefully detach the small offsets. Pot up in a sand and peat mix at a temperature of 21°C/70°F.

SPECIES *T. caput-medusae* has scrolled up grey foliage and crimson summer flowers. *T. fasciculata* has dark blue flowers and orange bracts. *T. recurvata* has blue/green flowers.

POSSIBLE PROBLEMS Generally trouble-free.

MIMOSA

| C | summer | sun | 60cm/24in | 30cm/12in |

Touch *M. pudica (above)*, the sensitive plant, and its leaves prompty fold up and the stem bends down to the ground. A hard-to-resist 'toy' which can be cut back for new growth, though it is never as effective second year round. Treat as an annual and discard.

GROWING Since there's just one season to build up a large specimen, it's worth producing the right conditions. Never let the soil dry out, feed weekly from early summer to early autumn, shade on scorching days, and spray regularly for high humidity. Tiny mauve flowers appear late in the summer.

PROPAGATION Germinate seeds at 18°C/65°F in early spring, and pot up when large enough to handle into 7.5cm/3in pots of John Innes No 1.

SPECIES Do not confuse this with the mimosa tree, *Acacia dealbata*, which, in its native Australia, grows to 7m/20ft and has scented yellowy flowers. It will not, sadly, perform tricks.

POSSIBLE PROBLEMS Generally trouble-free.

▪ GARDENER'S TIP

T. usneoides *needs to be grown as an epiphyte. Grow either on a piece of fallen tree branch or attach to a lengthy strip of bark. Compost is not required.*

▪ GARDENER'S TIP

If growing from seed select the five strongest plants and group together. This is invariably more visually impressive than one straggly mimosa, and *also makes quite an effect when you brush your hand across a wide mound of leaves and watch them close in a wave.*

ANNUAL & BEDDING PLANTS

Good gardeners are fascists. They're constantly re-assessing, deciding 'you live, you die'. So old plants, plants crippled by disease, plants flagging in the shade of more vigorous, splendid growers, plants with which one becomes thoroughly bored, all get tossed away. While there are spaces waiting for new long-term occupants to tuck their roots in and get established, annuals and bedding plants come into their own.

Neither are as popular as they once were, when money and labour were plentiful. Then, large estates might employ teams of gardeners 100 strong to spend hours flat on their stomachs lining up thousands of annuals, organizing them into intricate symbolic patterns. Today no one has the time and not often the inclination. However, every garden needs its scattering of annuals, and not just as temporary fillers. They set off the permanent stars with different scenery, shift the colour perspective, modify the atmosphere and emphasis, and more than anything give finger-happy gardeners extra things to do in the spring. Gardening has its rituals and the spring ritual of experimenting with trays and pots of new plants is one of the best.

BEDDING PLANTS Annual and bedding plants come in two basic types; hardy annuals and half-hardy annuals. The former include alyssum, *Centaurea cyanus* (cornflower), *Delphinium consolida* (larkspur; *see left*), godetia, helianthus (sunflower), *Nigella damascena* (love-in-a-mist), and lathyrus (sweet pea). The latter embrace antirrhinum, ipomoea (morning glory), lobelia, nicotiana (tobacco plant), petunia, tagetes (French marigold), and zinnia. While hardy annuals can be sown direct outside, they'll get off to a racing start in the greenhouse warmth. Frost-tender half-hardies must be sown within while there's any danger of frost.

SOWING To raise hardy annuals under glass, sow seeds in small pots of seed compost and water them in. Keep them shaded from direct sun, and take care not to overwater whilst not letting the compost dry right out. Keep an eye out for any seedlings which keel over, indicating damping off. When this occurs remove the affected seedlings immediately, and spray the remainder with chestnut compound or liquid copper.

PRICKING OUT AND GROWING ON When the seedlings are big enough to handle, prick them out into trays of seed compost, spacing them 5cm/2in apart. Handle them by the leaves, not the stems, to avoid bruising. Water them in and water again whenever the compost starts to feel on the dry side. Five weeks after pricking out the seedlings, regularly water with liquid or soluble feed, according to the manufacturer's instructions.

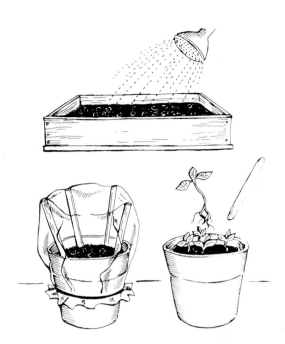

Sowing seed and pricking out

When the plants fill the tray harden them off for a couple of weeks by standing them outside during the day, and bringing them back under glass at night. Then they are ready to plant out. With hardy annuals you don't need to wait until there's no longer any danger of a frost, though it won't hurt if you do precisely that.

HALF-HARDY ANNUALS This category needs more warmth and can only be propagated with 100 per cent success in a heated greenhouse or heated propagator. Sow the seeds in the same way as for hardy annuals, then place the pot in the propagator at approximately 18°C/65°F. Gradually reduce the temperature when seedlings appear.

Prick out the larger seedlings into trays and return to the propagator for two more weeks and keep lowering the temperature. When the seedlings are almost touching each other you should have sufficiently hardened them off to stand them on the greenhouse staging where the temperature might be 5°C/40°F at night.

From now on grow them in exactly the same way as hardy annuals, but taking particular care to harden them off very thoroughly before planting them out. As they dislike cold weather, do not plant out half-hardy annuals until there is no more danger of a frost.

ANNUAL STYLE There's a tendency among gardeners to sniff at annuals as the lowest of the low. Yet they provide as much scent, shape and colour as any

A cottage garden display of a selection of brightly coloured flowers in a mixed border.

group. If you haven't grown a tobacco plant before, it is the one to try.

N. sylvestris has the best looks, with approximately a dozen, long thin tubular white flowers on each stem. It does justice to an ornamental pot and releases its scent at night. Grow *N. alata* in the shade and you might just trick it into thinking it's permanently night so you get more hours of fragrance. If grown in a sheltered bed, with an insulating protective mulch over winter, it might well survive a bad winter.

Other annuals deserve inclusion in any garden, whether cottage or formal, modern or seventeenth century, English, Italian or French. There's nothing to rival a brazen, giant sunflower, its face sprinting up to the tree tops, or a cluster of intensely coloured delphiniums, or an alyssum-packed stone wall which performs a quick change, rock one minute, the next grey turned startling white.

NIGELLA

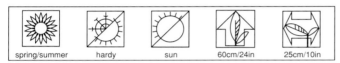

spring/summer	hardy	sun	60cm/24in	25cm/10in

Nigella is a versatile, reliable self-sowing annual. The bright foliage and heads of white, blue, red, or mauve flowers slot in with diverse shapes and colours. Use it in drifts in a chaotic cottage garden, or as the front line in a well-crafted, regimented border.

PROPAGATION Seeds germinated in the autumn produce larger, earlier flowers the following spring. Select the most vigorous seedlings every 15cm/6in or so, and set out in a sunny position. Refrain from hoeing round the plant if you want seedlings to cover bare patches.

SPECIES N. damascena (above), love-in-a-mist, is interesting for its autumn green and bronze seed heads. They hang among fine, fern-like foliage. 'Miss Jekyll Blue' has bright blue, semi-double flowers; 'Persian Jewels' is available in a wide colour range, mainly shades of blue and red. N. hispanica's flowers have the slightest scent and are followed by smaller seed heads. The red stamens make a good contrast with the foliage.

POSSIBLE PROBLEMS Generally trouble-free.

NICOTIANA

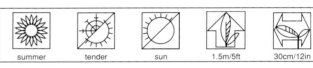

summer	tender	sun	1.5m/5ft	30cm/12in

The paler varieties of the tobacco plant invariably have the strongest, heady fragrance which is released in the evenings. The tallest species is N. sylvestris from the Andean foothills which grows to 1.5m/5ft. It's said to be coarse looking, but the scent is strong enough to fill the greenhouse. It can also be grown in a pot and brought indoors after sunset. The genus owes its common name to N. tabacum whose leaves are used in the tobacco industry.

PROPAGATION Germinate seed in early spring at a temperature of 18°C/65°F. Prick off the most vigorous seedlings and pot up in containers using John Innes No 2. The tallest varieties need staking, though N. sylvestris is quite sturdy. Water liberally and shelter from fierce sunlight.

SPECIES N. alata (above), is a half-hardy annual which will survive a mild winter, though it gets a bit straggly and is best replaced by spring plants; height 75cm/30in. N. suaveolens, also an annual, is smaller at 1m/3ft 3in and makes a good pot plant.

POSSIBLE PROBLEMS Aphids attack the young growth.

▧ CUT FLOWER TIP

Include the red-streaked seed pods in a flower arrangement of red, white and blue nigella. With the feathery foliage they give a surprise addition.

▧ GARDENER'S TIP

If you don't have a small bed by the front or back door it's well worth creating one and packing it with spring, summer and autumn scented plants. The

advantage of N. sylvestris for the high season is that it's tall and wafts its fragrance straight at you. You can't miss it.

ALYSSUM

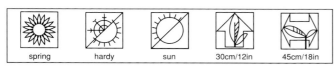

| spring | hardy | sun | 30cm/12in | 45cm/18in |

Grow either right at the front of a border, or more noticeably in a rock garden, on a wall, or between the cracks in a path. The strong colours make it a real attention grabber. Once planted it quickly takes hold. Alyssum are available as hardy annuals and perennials. *Alyssum saxatile (above)*, sometimes listed as *Aurinia saxatilis*, is a billowing clump of a perennial.

PROPAGATION Raise annuals by seed in early spring at a temperature of 13°C/55°F. Select the most vigorous seedlings, plant up in John Innes No 1 and harden off outside. Set out permanently in late spring. Perennials can be sown in a cold frame in mid-spring, hardened off over summer, and set out in early autumn.

Take 5cm/2in cuttings of perennials in early summer and insert in a sand and peat mix. Place in the cold frame, pot up singly, and set out the following spring.

SPECIES Other perennials include *A. argenteum* (yellow) and *A. montanum* (also yellow). *Alyssum saxatile* comes in a number of varieties - 'Citrinum' (pale lemon), 'Dudley Neville'(gold), and 'Flore-pleno' (double and yolk-yellow).

POSSIBLE PROBLEMS Slugs eat tender young shoots; mildew.

TAGETES

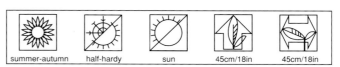

| summer-autumn | half-hardy | sun | 45cm/18in | 45cm/18in |

The French marigold, *T. patula*, is a half-hardy annual available in a wide colour range including bright orange and yellow (singles and doubles). This makes it the perfect plant for filling in gaps between staid shrubs grown for their architecture instead of their flowering potential.

PROPAGATION Germinate seeds in early spring at a temperature of 18°C/65°F. Harden off and set out a few weeks later in any soil, though the bed must be in a bright and sunny position. Deadhead for a better, longer flower display.

VARIETIES 'Fireflame' flowers in reds and yellows. 'Goldfinch', dark orange; 'Janie', pale orange; 'Naughty Marietta', yellow with an attractive maroon centre; 'Paprika', red, centred gold; 'Queen Sophie', russet-red laced gold; 'Suzie Wong', lemon; 'Tangerine Gem', orange.

POSSIBLE PROBLEMS Botrytis in damp, cold weather; foot rot.

■ GARDENER'S TIP

A small rock garden needs just a few plants to colonize it. Two alyssums with iberis, several varieties of saxifraga, and arabis will quickly dominate the scene.

Even better they require the minimum amount of attention, apart from the occasional deadheading.

■ GARDENER'S TIP

It's claimed that if you plant marigolds in among your most precious flowers they'll keep them healthy. Whitefly apparently dislike the scent and weeds can't

stand the root chemicals. Since scientists haven't disproved the theory it is certainly worth having a go.

ZINNIA

| summer | half-hardy | sun | 60cm/24in | 30cm/12in |

The Mexican native *Z. elegans (above)* comes in a variety of pompom and dahlia-like shapes and colours, from lime green to salmon pink, and makes good cut flowers. Like other zinnia annuals, and the perennials, it needs a long dry summer to excel. Heavy rainfall ruins the flowers. Don't plant them all out in one go in case the weather kills the display and you're left with a toothy gap in the border. Keep some in the greenhouse in reserve.

PROPAGATION Germinate seeds at 18°C/65°F in early spring. Prick out into peat pots and, after hardening off, set out without disturbing the roots. Free-draining soil in a sunny position is ideal, with some shelter from the worst weather. Pinch out when young for extra bushiness and regularly deadhead.

VARIETIES *Z. e.* has dozens of strains and hybrids. They include 'Belvedere Dwarfs' and Burpee hybrids, both fast growing and in various colours; 'Canary Bird', yellow; 'Envy', lime green; and the Ruffles series, scarlet.

POSSIBLE PROBLEMS Botrytis attacks the seedlings.

HELIANTHUS

| summer | hardy | sun | 3m/10ft | 45cm/18in |

The annual giant sunflower, *H. annuus*, comes from the Americas. The face-size disc, within the yellow rays, produces the seed used in the production of sunflower oil.

PROPAGATION Germinate seeds in spring at a temperature of 16°C/61°F and raise in small pots of John Innes No 1. After hardening off two months later plant out in free-draining soil in a sheltered site. Later, tie-in to tall stakes if in an exposed, windy area.

VARIETIES 'Russian Giant' is one of the tallest, reaching 3m/10ft. 'Italian White' (1.2m/4ft tall) has cream flowers. 'Orange Sun Double' grows to 90cm/36in. Dwarf sunflowers include 'Sunspot', 60cm/24in, and 'Music Box' which grows marginally higher.

POSSIBLE PROBLEMS Botrytis can be quite a problem during long, damp spells.

GARDENER'S TIP

Z. angustifolia *'Persian Carpet'* is the best plant to withstand a bad summer. It's 38cm/15in high and has bi-coloured, double flowers.

GROWING TIP

It's well worth growing sunflowers if only to see whether you can beat the record height. Grow one tall variety in a particularly warm place and feed well.

NEMESIA

| summer | half-hardy | sun | 15-30cm/6in-12in | 15cm/6om |

The South African *N. strumosa (above)* is a good multi-purpose plant with bright 2.5cm/1in flowers. Grow it in formal bedding schemes, topsy-turvy cottage gardens, or in greenhouse pots. It's one of the best half-hardy annuals.

PROPAGATION Sow thin scatterings of seed in early spring at a temperature of 15-18°C/60-65°F. Thin to 5cm/2in and harden off outside in late spring. Beware of letting the soil dry out or extreme temperature fluctuations because a check to growth results in spindly, weedy plants. For a greenhouse 20cm/8in pot, grow four plants in John Innes No 2. Pinch out all young plants to increase bushiness.

VARIETIES *N. strumosa* 'Blue Gem' has sky blue flowers (23cm/9in), 'Mello' has red and white flowers, 'Tapestry' comes in a wide colour range of upright, bushy plants, and includes orange, yellow, lilac, white and dark red.

POSSIBLE PROBLEMS Root rot can be a problem.

CALENDULA

| spring-autumn | hardy | sun | 60cm/24in | 30cm/12in |

C. officinalis (above), the pot marigold, differs from *Tagetes patula*, the French marigold, in three key respects. It's a native of southern Europe, not Mexico; it's a hardy annual, not half-hardy; and it grows to approximately twice the height. The flowers are similar but those of pot marigolds are slightly more compact. Both make excellent bedding plants.

PROPAGATION Germinate seeds in autumn (for an outdoor spring display), or the following spring to flower months later. Thin out to prevent overcrowding and plant virtually anywhere. Pot marigolds are not fussy, but ideally they enjoy a free-draining soil neither too light nor rich and heavy.

VARIETIES Tall varieties (over 45cm/18in): 'Art Shades' comes in apricot, orange and cream; 'Kablouna Gold', chocolate coloured; 'Sunglow', bright yellow. Dwarf varieties (up to 30cm/12in): 'Apricot Bon Bon' (warm apricot); 'Fiesta Gitana' (all colours).

POSSIBLE PROBLEMS Mildew; rust.

■ GARDENER'S TIP

For a second flowering cut back the stems once the first display declines. This is really worthwhile with greenhouse pots, the flowers will last well into autumn. N. strumosa's flowers are particularly suitable for a fresh flower arrangement.

■ GARDENING TIP

The most vigorous autumn-sown plants can be moved to containers filled with John Innes No 2, and then brought indoors. The bright, strong colours and large-headed flowers make an excellent Christmas display.

CELOSIA

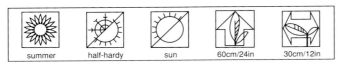

| summer | half-hardy | sun | 60cm/24in | 30cm/12in |

A summer-flowering annual: *C. argentea cristata* known as cockscomb, is highly regarded for its unusual, feathery, upright flowers.

PROPAGATION In spring sow the seeds at a temperature of 16°C/61°F in 7.5cm/3in pots. Scatter a few in each and thin out to the strongest seedling. When the roots are putting on good growth begin to liquid feed. Pot up to 9cm/3½in pots. The first priority is sunlight, followed by regular, ample watering. Never allow the compost to dry out. Once the flower display is over the plants can be discarded.

SPECIES *C. argentea* has white flowers and grows to 60cm/24in. Varieties *(above)* come in a wide range of colours. *C. a. lumosa* is slightly shorter at 45cm/18in and has yellow flowers. Cockscomb grows to 30cm/12in.

POSSIBLE PROBLEMS Frequent spraying with water should keep thrips and red spider at bay.

LATHYRUS

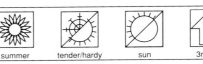

| summer | tender/hardy | sun | 3m/10ft | 30cm/12in |

Modern varieties of *L. odoratus (above)*, the sweet pea, feature colour and size at the expense of scent. But the older kinds are still available. There's a great deal of conflicting advice about the best way to grow sweet pea. The latest research goes as follows.

PROPAGATION Show specimens for mild-climate gardens can be sown in situ in the autumn. For cottage garden displays, and colder areas, sow in the spring under glass. Before planting quickly rub the seeds on a sheet of sandpaper to let water in and speed up germination. Next, fill a small but deep peat pot with John Innes No 1, water, and plant three seeds. Raise at 15°C/60°F and thin to the strongest shoot in each pot. Gradually harden off in a sunny position and then plant out. For prize specimens remove all tendrils and side growth, concentrating the plant's energy on its bloom. Tie in to a stake. In all other cases leave the tendrils which attach themselves to fences, etc. A wigwam of canes saves space.

SPECIES *L. odoratus* has many different varieties including dwarf (height from 45cm/18in to 1.2m/4ft), and giant (3m/10ft). Two everlasting, perennial sweet peas are *L. latifolius* and *L. rotundifolius*.

POSSIBLE PROBLEMS Aphids; mildew; slugs.

▪ GARDENER'S TIP

It's definitely worth sowing extra pots from which to make a final selection. A group of the very best rejects can be given away as presents.

▪ SPECIAL CARE TIP

The young shoots are held in high regard by birds who flock to eat them. In the open, cover with netting for the first few weeks.

SCHIZANTHUS

| summer | half-hardy | sun | 1.2m/4ft | 20cm/8in |

The annual schizanthus is more popularly known as the butterfly flower and poor man's orchid. *S. pinnatus (above)*, like *S. × wisetonensis*, has highly ornamental flowers which are ideal for growing in pots and using as cut flowers. There are numerous varieties in a wide colour range.

PROPAGATION Germinate the seeds in late summer at a temperature of 16°C/61°F. Select the most vigorous seedlings and pot up into 7.5cm/3in pots. When they are 10cm/4in high pinch out for extra bushiness. When growing outside, sow the seeds in spring, harden off the plants in a cold frame, and later plant in the border. *S. pinnatus*, which is the taller species (1.2m/4ft), needs cane support. Schizanthus prefers a rich soil in full sun.

VARIETIES 'Giant Hybrids' are the tallest at 1.2m/4ft. 'Dwarf Bouquet' grows to 38cm/15in. 'Star Parade' is one of the smallest at 23cm/9in.

POSSIBLE PROBLEMS Aphids attack the growing tips.

TROPAEOLUM

| summer | hardy | shade | 3m/10ft | 90cm/36in |

The genus includes many excellent 'lightweight' climbers. The best are *T. majus*, the annual yellow and orange flowering common nasturtium from South America, which readily scrambles up through other shrubs; *T. speciosum (above)*, a perennial, which has sensational flame red bloom and increases via underground rhizomes; and *T. tuberosum* 'Ken Aslet', again a perennial, with red and yellow flowers. *T. tuberosum* doesn't flower until the end of the season.

PROPAGATION Germinate annual seeds in early spring at a temperature of 15°C/60°F. Transplant seedlings to 7.5cm/3in pots of John Innes No 2 and harden off before planting outside in late spring. Or, grow in a hanging basket so the stems can trail over the side.

Plant tubers (*T. s.* and *T. tuberosum*) in free-draining, good soil in a sunny position. Get them off to an early spring start in a greenhouse pot. Transfer to a place where the lower growth will be in the shade of a shrub.

SPECIES Other annuals include *T. peltophorum*, height 1.8m/6ft; *T. peregrinum* (the canary creeper), height 3.6m/12ft. Perennial: *T. tricolor*, height 1.2m/4ft.

POSSIBLE PROBLEMS Aphids.

▪ GARDENER'S TIP

A small pot is unbeatable when containing one of each of the different varieties, say five in all. Species mixing can be disastrous, but not here.

▪ SPECIAL CARE TIP

Nasturtiums dislike too rich a soil. If you over feed them you'll get a massive show of foliage and very few flame coloured flowers.

SALVIA

| summer-autumn | hardy/tender | sun | 1.5m/5ft | 1.2m/4ft |

A highly varied genus which includes sage, showy summer bedding plants, and tender species with exotic colours. Two of the best scented are *S. rutilans* which flowers red at Christmas and whose leaves smell exactly like pineapple, and *S. discolor* which smells of blackcurrants.

PROPAGATION Germinate seeds of annuals in early spring. Raise at a temperature of 18°C/65°F, and harden off two months later. Set out in free-draining soil in a sunny site, and pinch out the young plants to induce extra bushiness. The perennials are seed sown in mid-spring and either set out in their final position that autumn, or the following spring. They need much richer soil. Once established they can be divided over winter.

SPECIES The annual *S. horminium* flowers in mauves and pinks on upright, 45cm/18in high stems. *S. splendens (above)* is slightly shorter and flowers in various bright colours until cut down by frost.

POSSIBLE PROBLEMS Red spider mites.

SALPIGLOSSIS

| spring-autumn | half-hardy | sun | 60cm/24in | 25cm/10in |

S. sinuata (above) produces abundant, showy, fast-growing, trumpet-like flowers. The petals are silky, the stems sticky, the bloom multi-coloured. Extra seeds are well worth saving for an ornamental pot which can be brought indoors in full bloom.

PROPAGATION Germinate seeds in early spring at a temperature of 18°C/65°F. Prick out and harden off in late spring for planting out soon after. Set out in moderately rich soil, and on exposed sites support with canes. Regularly deadhead for bushier, free-flowering plants. Pot-grown salpiglossis needs John Innes No 2 above a thick layer of drainage material.

VARIETIES 'Kew Blue' has rich blue flowers with clear gold veins (height 30cm/1ft). 'Bolero', 'Casino', and 'Splash' are available in various colours.

POSSIBLE PROBLEMS Aphids gorge on the stems; fungus leads to foot rot and plant wilting.

▦ GARDENING TIP

S. rutilans *can be grown outside over summer, where it requires regular watering. Dig up and put in a large pot to bring indoors for winter-flowering. The* pineapple *leaves can be used in salads or fruit cocktails. An established plant will yield scores of cuttings which root incredibly quickly.*

▦ CUT FLOWER TIP

Salpiglossis mix well with alstroemeria. They have similar deep blooms flaring different colours. The latter are neater, the former refreshingly brash.

ANTIRRHINUM

| summer | hardy | sun | 90cm/36in | 45cm/18in |

Tall antirrhinum (*A. majus* – hardy annuals) are ideal for the middle row of the border. They've got height, are supported by surrounding plants, and have long stems of flower that last up to the first frost. Squeeze the flowers and they look like the open jaws of a dragon, hence the common name, snapdragon.

PROPAGATION Early spring-sown seed (at 18°C/65°F) produces plants for hardening off three months later and setting out shortly after. They like rich, quick-draining soil in an open sunny position. Pinch out when 10cm/4in high for extra side growth unless you want cut flowers, in which case leave single stems. Deadhead right through summer. Antirrhinum can also be grown as pot plants with four per 30cm/12in container. For early flowering sow in mid-summer, harden off outside in the autumn, and bring back under glass as the temperature cools down.

VARIETIES There are three groups categorized by size. Tall (60cm/24in and over) – 'Bright Butterfly', 'Coronette', and the series 'Supreme'. Medium (30-60cm/12-24in) – 'Madame Butterfly', 'His Excellency', and the Monarch series. Low (up to 30cm/12in) – 'Little Darling', 'Little Gem Mixed', and 'Pixie'.

POSSIBLE PROBLEMS Mildew causes stunted growth. Rust creates dark brown leaf pustules. Aphids.

DIANTHUS

| summer | hardy | sun | 60cm/24in | 25cm/10in |

D. barbatus, sweet William, is an early summer-flowering biennial typically found in cottage gardens. It has a distinct scent, though hardly pervasive, and makes tasteful, dense groupings of velvety cut flowers. Other species include carnations and pinks *(see page 34)*, many with much stronger and more gorgeous scent.

PROPAGATION Germinate seeds in early spring at a temperature of 13°C/55°F. Harden off and plant out in late spring. Remember to sow seeds two years running for an annual display. Set out in free-draining, moderate soil with applications of lime in the case of acid ground.

VARIETIES There are several named varieties and many hybrids. The Roundabout series is 15cm/6in high whereas the Monarch series is three times taller, and much bushier.

POSSIBLE PROBLEMS Carnation ring spot results in grey spots. At its worst the disease wipes out the entire plant, stems, foliage and flowers.

■ SPECIAL CARE TIP

Rust is a major problem with antirrhinum. Always grow rust-resistant varieties and, if you do spot the symptoms, destroy all infected stock.

■ GARDENING TIP

Sweet William come in mixed colours so if you spot one which you'd like more of, strip away the flower heads and use the side shoots as cuttings.

MESMBRYANTHEMUM

spring/summer	hardy	sun	15cm/6in	15cm/6in

A succulent hardy annual for the 'hot-and-dry' border and rock garden. The packed mass of low-growing, daisy-like flowers with button centres only perform on sunny days. When it's cloudy they stay firmly shut. The colour range is huge, running from flamingo-pink to crimson. Note that mesembryanthemum is often listed as dorotheanthus.

PROPAGATION Germinate seeds in spring at 15°C/60°F. Harden off the most vigorous in late spring, and plant out several weeks later in free-draining, sandy soil.

SPECIES *M. criniflorum* syn. *Dorotheanthus bellidiformis*, the Livingstone daisy from South Africa, is a good colonizing plant, spreading across the ground at a height of 15cm/6in with its brash flowers. M. 'Tricolor' syn. *D. gramineus*, is even smaller at just 7.5cm/3in.

POSSIBLE PROBLEMS Foot rot can be a hazard.

GODETIA

spring/summer	hardy	sun	60cm/24in	15cm/6in

The most popular species is *G. grandiflora* (commonly listed as clarkia). It's robust and compact, flowers in singles or doubles, and in a wide colour range from early summer. The vivid bloom is offset by the neat green leaves.

PROPAGATION Sow seeds in the autumn and keep under glass over winter for planting out the following spring. Thin seedlings to a distance of 15cm/6in. Alternatively germinate seeds in early spring for flowering that summer.

Outside, these annuals require a free-draining soil, and plenty of water during dry spells. If the soil is too rich the plant puts its energy into leaf, instead of flower production.

VARIETIES 'Cattleya' has pink flowers, 'Crystal Palace' light blue, 'Firelight' rich crimson, 'Kelvedon Glory' flame orange and 'Sybil Sherwood' pale pink. 'Crimson Glow' *(above)* is a dwarf plant.

POSSIBLE PROBLEMS Botrytis is one likely cause of root and stem rot which results in severe wilting.

■ SPECIAL CARE TIP

Foot rot is caused by too much wet soil round the roots. Once you spot the problem rectify immediately by transplanting to another stonier part of the garden where rainwater quickly drains away. Do not even consider growing mesembryanthemum on heavy clay soil.

■ GARDENING TIP

There's no reason why you shouldn't have godetia flowering at Christmas, even well into the New Year. Save a handful of seed and sow in late summer in 15cm/6in pots filled with seed compost. Select the most vigorous seedling in each container and remove the rest.

LOBELIA

| spring/summer | half-hardy | sun | 90cm/36in | 23cm/9in |

Trailing lobelia are traditionally reserved for the hanging basket, though they look equally good at the front of the border flowering hither and thither among other plants. Tall and small kinds come in a wide range of sharp colours. *L. erinus* (height 15cm/6in), and *L. tenuior* (height 30cm/12in) are both perennials grown as annuals.

PROPAGATION Germinate seeds in early spring at 18°C/65°F. Thin down to the most vigorous shoots, reduce the temperature, and harden off in late spring. A continuous sowing and regular deadheading gives a long summer's display.

SPECIES The compact varieties of *L. erinus* include: 'Cambridge Blue', 'Mrs Clibran', and 'Snowball'. Trailing varieties: 'Red Cascade', and 'Sapphire'. *L. tenuior* is particularly suitable for winter-flowering pots. Other perennials include *L. fulgens* and *L. siphilitica*, both of which grow to 90cm/36in. *L. × vedrariense (above)*, grows slightly higher.

POSSIBLE PROBLEMS Damping off and stem rot makes the plants wilt and eventually collapse.

IPOMOEA

| summer | half-hardy | sun | 3m/10ft | 30cm/12in |

Three species are grown as annuals including *I. purpurea*, morning glory (so named because the purple flowers are at their glorious best early in the day, and fade with the afternoon). Though these climbers can be grown outside in a warm bed, they also make exceptional plants for ornamental pots.

PROPAGATION Germinate the seeds in mid-spring at a minimum of 15°C/60°F or the seedling will gradually die. Transplant two young plants to an 7.5cm/3in pot filled with John Innes No 1, pinch out, and later transfer to a 20cm/8in pot with John Innes No 2. Stand against a trellis so the growth can be tied in. Outside, plant in a free-draining, rich soil against a warm, sunny wall for support.

SPECIES Half-hardy annuals: *I. coccinea* has scented, scarlet flowers (height 3m/10ft); *I. purpurea* grows to 3m/10ft; *I. quamoclit* has orange flowers (height 1.8m/6ft), *I. tricolor (above)* has purple-blue flowers (height 2.4m/8ft). Perennials are also available: *I. lobata* syn. *Mina lobata* is so tender it's often grown as an annual. The same is true of *I. violacea* which has lilac flowers (height 2.4m/8ft).

POSSIBLE PROBLEMS Aphids attack the tender young shoots.

■ SPECIAL CARE TIP

L. f. is a half-hardy and needs to be protected over winter. Use either a cloche to keep out the cold or a deep insulating mulch of leaves and bracken.

■ GARDENING TIP

Blue and red coloured ipomoea make an excellent contrast when grown with climbing, scented yellow honeysuckle, a white rose and pink clematis. Entwine

all three round a wooden pillar, across a pergola, or better still around the entrance to a porch.

PETUNIA

| spring/summer | half-hardy | sun | 30cm/12in | 30cm/12in |

The blue and purple petunias have the best evening scent. The genus thrives in good summers, and is traditionally grown in all kinds of ornamental containers from hanging baskets to free-standing chimney pots, but can be ruined by a chilly wet season. 'Resisto Mixed' is the best strain for withstanding bad weather on exposed sites.

PROPAGATION   Germinate seeds in early spring at 15°C/60°F and harden off seedlings before setting out. Plant in light soil in full sun. Too rich a soil in too dark a situation results in foliage instead of flowers. For pot plants use John Innes No 1.

VARIETIES   There are four groups. Multifloras are bushy prodigious flowerers and include scores of F_1 hybrids like 'Blue Skies' (light blue) and 'Bumble' (ginger). Grandifloras have larger, fewer flowers. They include 'Californian Girl' (yolk-yellow) and 'Razzle-Dazzle' (in various colours). The final two groups are Nana Compacta (15cm/6in high), and Pendula whose trailing stems are ideal for hanging baskets.

POSSIBLE PROBLEMS   Aphids feed on the tender young shoots.

BROWALLIA

| summer | half-hardy | sun | 60cm/24in | 30cm/12in |

A South American annual grown for a mass flower display right through summer. It can only be raised outside in the mildest areas.

PROPAGATION   Sow in John Innes No 1 at 18°C/65°F in early spring. Pot up singly and regularly pinch out to create a small, compact bush. Eventually move into a 12.5cm/5in container. For a Christmas-flowering plant delay seed sowing until mid-summer. Give a weak liquid feed when the flower buds begin to swell.

SPECIES   *B. speciosa (above)* has bright green leaves and violet coloured flowers. *B. s. major* is the largest form and can exceed 90cm/36in if grown in the greenhouse border. Grown in a pot, with its roots restricted, it is unlikely to reach any higher than 60cm/24in. The bright violet-blue flowers should last until mid-autumn. 'Silver Bells' is a small variety at half the height and flowers white. *B. demissa* comes in two varieties, with white, and blue flowers. *B. viscosa*'s flowers are blue with a white centre.

POSSIBLE PROBLEMS   Generally trouble-free.

◼ SPECIAL CARE TIP

One way to prevent critical aphid attacks in the green-house involves hanging up a special, glue-coated board near the seedlings. The aphids can't resist it.

◼ GARDENER'S TIP

For a Christmas present with a real difference sow seeds of three different varieties. Plant the strongest seedling of each into the same pot.

DELPHINIUM

spring/summer	hardy	sun	1.2m/4ft	30cm/12in

Annual delphiniums are popularly known as larkspur. They are quintessential cottage plants, tall, lean and cheery over a full season. The colour range includes everything from blue to crimson. They also make excellent cut flowers.

PROPAGATION Sow the seeds in autumn for early spring flowering, or in spring to flower a few months later. Plant out in rich, free-draining soil, with taller varieties preferably in a sheltered position though the spikes will need staking in any event. Don't let the soil dry round the roots.

SPECIES *D. ajacis*, rocket larkspur, grows to 90cm/36in and should be spaced at 30cm/12in intervals. At least two thirds of the stem is covered with flowers. Good for cutting. The small form is 30cm/12in high. *D. consolida*, larkspur, grows to 1.2m/4ft in the Giant Imperial strain. For cut flowers use Stock-flowered plants. The perennials include *D. cardinale* and *D. elatum*. The latter lasts longer and can be increased by division.

POSSIBLE PROBLEMS Fungus attack leads to black root, crown, and root rot. Also look out for botrytis.

CENTAUREA

spring/summer	hardy	sun	90cm/36in	30cm/12in

C. cyanus, the cornflower, is a middle-of-the-border annual which can vary in height from 30cm/12in to 90cm/36in. It requires little staking, has varieties flowering in white, red, pink, purple, and blue, and makes excellent cut flowers. Dwarf forms are also available for the front of the border or pots.

PROPAGATION Germinate the seeds in early autumn. Sow in John Innes No 1 in a frost-free greenhouse, harden off early next spring and plant out soon after in rich, free-draining soil. Further sowings that spring will give a longer flower display. Perennial species (eg *C. dealbata*, *C. macrocephala*, and *C. pulchra*) are sown in spring, hardened off over summer, and set out in early autumn. They can be divided the following autumn.

VARIETIES Tall: *C. cyanus* 'Black Ball' is chocolate coloured, appearing black on dark days; height 75cm/30in. 'Pink Ball' (pink), is the same height. Dwarf: *C. c. nana* 'Jubilee Gem' *(above)* has blue flowers; height 25cm/10in. The Polka Dot series comes in a wide colour range, and is slightly taller at 38cm/15in.

POSSIBLE PROBLEMS Mildew; rust.

■ GARDENER'S TIP

If you live in an open, upland garden then no amount of staking is going to prevent the taller varieties getting flayed by racing winds. If this is the case, it's best to try the smaller varieties. Like all delphinium they need to be protected from slug damage. Use an organic powder.

■ ORGANIC TIP

Groups of cornflower planted round the garden ensure a plentiful supply of bees and other insects. They cannot resist the strong-scented nectar.

FRUIT

Cold greenhouses are fine for most fruit, but with extra heat the range, and the chance of early crops, increases. When the weather is unseasonable start cheating by keeping all doors and windows closed, providing extra warmth with a special paraffin heater. Ventilate well when outside temperatures pick up again. To ensure a warm-as-possible greenhouse, position it in a sheltered, sunny spot.

Greenhouse length also counts. Fan-shape peaches and apricots need to be a minimum of 5.5m/15ft apart, and the best solution is a long lean-to against a heat-retaining stone wall. When growing grapes you have the option of planting the roots outside, threading the stems through a small hole in the side of the green-house wall enabling the fruit to ripen under glass. Wherever you create extra space in the border plant up with strawberries which, with initial temperatures of 10-13°C/50-55°F, will give a splendid early crop. With heat they will be ready to eat in early spring.

STARTING WITH GOOD SOIL This is crucial. Dig in well-rotted manure, and with lumpy, gluey, albeit nutritious clay add mushroom compost as a soil conditioner. Outside, frost breaks up the clods; under glass it's up to you.

Soil conditioning also guarantees good drainage. This is improved with scatterings of broken terracotta pot, horticultural grit, etc. Fruit trees particularly dislike having their roots locked in airless, solid wet soil and quickly develop root rot and canker which no spraying programme will ever cure.

SUPPORT AND PROTECTION During a good summer the greenhouse door is going to be open most of the time. Birds won't flock in, but you'll get the occasional visitor who'll quickly devour what's on offer. Cut out a strip of nylon mesh and attach the width of each end to a cane. The top one rests in a pair of curved hooks above the door, the bottom cane lies on the ground. Over winter you roll it up and store away.

Lean-to greenhouses against stone walls, should be annually cleaned and the rough surfaces whitewashed. This eliminates pests and increases the amount of reflected light. Next, create a taut criss-cross of wires against the wall so that apricots, figs, grapes, melons, peaches, etc, can be tied in. This stops the plant becoming a tangled mess, enables you to spot and easily treat pests and diseases should they strike, and ensures all parts of the plant get the maximum amount of sunlight. The fruit develop to their maximum size and are easily picked.

To create the wire structure attach battens running the height of the greenhouse at 1.8m/6ft intervals, with horizontal wires (14 gauge) fixed to vine eyes. They should be spaced 45cm/18in apart. Alternatively, the eyes can be drilled directly into the greenhouse frame. A quicker method involves buying sheets of netting, though avoid the plastic kind since they rarely last more than three years.

INITIAL FAN SHAPES FOR PEACH AND NECTARINE

The initial process is finickety, but gives fine results. The four stages are:

FIRST YEAR Prune the vertical stem 60cm/24in above soil level in early spring, leaving one bud to either side. Later, as these buds develop tie each to a 30cm/12in long cane, the latter being tied-in at an upward angle of 45 degrees to the background wires. Rub out any buds below this V-shape.

SECOND YEAR In early spring prune the two growths to 45cm/18in. Later that summer leave the two most vigorous shoots on the top side of both branches and train at an upward angle of 70 degrees, again along a cane. Train one shoot from the underside, growing it horizontally away from the main stem, which in turn is allowed to continue growing. Rub out all other shoots.

THIRD YEAR In early spring prune all eight growths back to a maximum length of 75cm/30in, each cut made just above a bud. That summer leave the main stems to grow, and allow just three vigorous buds per branch (two above, one below) to develop along canes. Towards the end of summer stop the fruit-bearing growth of these stems at 45cm/18in and tie to canes.

REMAINING YEARS Rub out all inward and outward growing buds to maintain the basic fan shape. Note that by tying all new growth to canes you create a clean, symmetrical shape. The canes are removed when the branches are stiff and woody.

POLLINATION

When flowers appear early in the year, before the appearance of insects (which might not in any event enter the greenhouse in large numbers), pollinate by hand. Dab the pollen with a small brush and transfer from flower to flower. This is particularly necessary with early strawberries.

FRUIT TREES IN POTS

Gardening is so time consuming the less potwork you've got the better. It's generally best to devote this aspect to highly scented and/or brilliantly coloured tender plants. Nonetheless, it may be worthwhile growing a pair of fruit trees in a container. Pears, plums, gages, etc, can be over-

In a lean-to greenhouse peaches thrive when grown against a heat retaining wall. It is also an ideal site to train the plant into a fan shape.

wintered under glass where they will put on good growth, before being stood out for the summer. Fruit trees in pots can also be an architectural asset. Impose shape on the shapeless, pruning in spring when the sap is rising to avoid the spread of infection.

Plant up in the autumn into a 38cm/15in pot (with John Innes No 2), this should sustain a fruiting tree for several years. Once the plant is a sturdy little specimen remove from the pot, brush away the lose soil in mid-spring without breaking up the root ball, and fill in with John Innes No 3. Always provide excellent drainage using stones, pebbles, and broken crocks.

Finally check the strength of the pot. Even a dwarf tree's root system can warp or split a weak container. Terracotta should eliminate the problem, but you must still carry out annual renovation. In mid-spring remove the plant and clear the drainage holes, pruning back any long fleshy roots to encourage the formation of compact, fibrous roots.

BANANA TREE

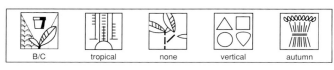

| B/C | tropical | none | vertical | autumn |

An excellent architectural plant and good fun to grow though not all varieties produce edible fruit. *Musa cavendishii* is a reliable fruiter for the humid, tropical greenhouse and grows to 2.1m/7ft high x 1.5m/5ft.

GROWING Raise either in 30cm/12in pots filled with John Innes No 3, or in the border soil enriched with humus. Over winter the minimum temperatures of 10°C/50°F are required (when little watering is necessary), increasing in summer to 21°C/70°F (when extra water must be provided). Feed with a liquid fertilizer from early spring to late autumn. Since tender new foliage is prone to sun-scorching the greenhouse needs to be shaded. Bananas raised in containers also need to be inspected regularly to avoid becoming pot-bound. This particularly applies to young specimens, and plants putting on good growth may have to be repotted twice a year. *M. basjoo* (yellow flowers) and *M. ensete* (reddish-green flowers) will grow in a cool greenhouse, even outside in mild areas, though without fruiting.

HARVESTING *M. c.* fruits in the autumn.

POSSIBLE PROBLEMS Generally trouble-free.

MELON

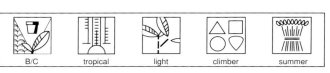

| B/C | tropical | light | climber | summer |

They are far more easily grown than is popularly believed. The one essential requirement is a 2.1m/7ft high greenhouse. Success is possible in a cold greenhouse but with artificial heat the results will be far better.

GROWING Sow seed in early spring for early/mid-summer fruit. Use 7.5cm/3in pots of seed compost covered with cling film. Remove when growth appears and provide a minimum temperature of 18°C/65°F. In the cold greenhouse sow seed inside a heated propagator, timing removal of the seedling to coincide with fine summer temperatures. The bed must be mounded to a height of 30cm/12in and fertilized with Growmore and a scattering of bonemeal. Provide vertical wire supports to the roof. Plant up, pinching out growing tips at 1.5m/5ft to encourage laterals which in turn must be stopped at five leaves. The resultant side shoots bear the fruit. Stop the latter growth at two leaves after the flowers, and limit each plant to five melons. Pollinate by hand and give adequate ventilation when temperatures exceed 23°C/73°F.

HARVESTING Press your finger tips into the top of the melon. When the fruit gently yields it is ripe.

POSSIBLE PROBLEMS Whitefly; red spider mite, mildew.

■ GARDENER'S TIP

A banana tree can be propagated by removing suckers at the base once flowering has ceased. Transfer to a 9cm/3½in pot of John Innes No 1 and maintain at 21°C/70°F. Alternatively grow from seed in April at similar temperatures.

■ GARDENER'S TIP

To prevent large, heavy melons on climbing varieties from falling prematurely, give support. Collect string onion bags, or pieces of old netting, and tie the four corners to the roof. The melon rests inside, as a trapeze artist is held by a safety net.

GRAPE

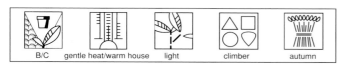

B/C	gentle heat/warm house	light	climber	autumn

To avoid a vine taking over the greenhouse roof, restrict size of certain varieties by growing as a 1.2m/4ft high container standard.

GROWING Insert good drainage material in the soil and prepare wires running the length of the roof for tying-in. In spring prune the vine to 15cm/6in above the soil, cutting just above a leaf joint. Select the three most vigorous new shoots and remove the rest. On reaching 1.5m/5ft high pinch out the growing tips and allow new side shoots to develop three leaves before pinching out. This pruning programme is vital for creating a strong framework. During the growing period water well with a liquid fertilizer, reducing both when the autumn foliage falls. Every winter cut back each stem to 20cm/8in from the main trunk. From the second year on let the leading buds grow unhindered, unless growth is too prolific. Although flowers and fruit will develop in the second year, there won't be a decent crop until the third.

POSSIBLE PROBLEMS Lack of ventilation and high humidity lead to mildew.

VARIETIES Black grapes: 'Lady Hastings' (early); 'Black Hamburgh' (mid-season); 'West's St. Peter's' (late). White grapes: 'Royal Muscadine' (early); 'Muscat of Hungary' (mid-season); 'Golden Queen' (late).

▓ GARDENER'S TIP

To save space in the border, plant outside right next to the greenhouse. Cut a circular hole in the wall about the size of a tennis ball. Lead the stems through and into the warmth of the greenhouse where the fruit will ripen. This technique can also be used with a conservatory.

FIG

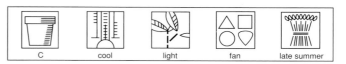

C	cool	light	fan	late summer

Specimens don't have to grow big to provide fruit. When a container grown plant reaches the height of 90cm/36in, it will produce a perfectly decent crop. While you can use outdoor varieties ('Brown Turkey'), those specifically for the greenhouse ('White Marseilles' and 'Rouge de Bordeaux') yield better quality fruit. The height of a mature specimen should be approximately 3m/10ft x 4.5m/15ft.

GROWING In spring select a bushy young plant. Transfer to a larger container, if pot-bound, filled with John Innes No 3. Give minimum amounts of water until several new leaves appear, and then increase. Prune in winter only to remove damaged shoots and prevent excessive overcrowding. By the time figs appear on the shoot tips the plant will need quite heavy watering, particularly on hot days when up to 4.5 litres / 1 gallon will be required. If you let the soil dry out the fruit will fall. After harvesting the leaves fall and watering virtually ceases.

HARVESTING Pick the fruit when very soft; it should easily come away from the tree. Note that a crop ripens over a four- to six-week period.

POSSIBLE PROBLEMS Botrytis on young shoots leads to dieback. The fungus can also attack the fruit which will then rot or fall prematurely.

▓ GARDENER'S TIP

Figs thrive when their root system is cramped. Don't use anything larger than a 50cm/20in pot otherwise the plant will put on excessive amounts of jungly, leafy growth instead of fruit-bearing shoots. Remove each autumn and trim back roots by 10 per cent.

APRICOT

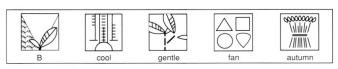

B	cool	gentle	fan	autumn

A greenhouse is essential since the early spring blossom needs frost protection and the end-of-summer fruit needs constant warmth to ripen. Because trees are too big for the traditional greenhouse, grow in a lean-to against a sunny wall or alternatively use a semi-dwarfing variety, which can reach a height of 2.4m/8ft x 3.6m/12ft.

GROWING Apricots can be grown in pots for the first few years, but they have such active root growth and so large an appetite that they quickly out-grow their containers and are better suited to the greenhouse border. Fan-trained trees are good space-savers. Plant a two- to three-year-old tree in mid-winter in soil which was well-manured the previous autumn. Water in and feed occasionally over summer with a liquid fertilizer. In the second year prune by one third for more compact growth and extra fruit. Pollinate by hand since there will be few active insects at this time of year. By thinning fruitlets to 15cm/6in in early summer quality improves. Over winter the plant needs cool conditions, approximately 4°C/39°F, and soil on the dry side.

HARVESTING The fruit should be ready in late summer, depending on variety. Pick seven days after they have reached a plump yellowness. Remove with a gentle tug.

POSSIBLE PROBLEMS Peach leaf curl, aphids.

LEMON

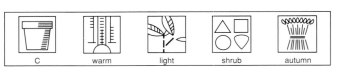

C	warm	light	shrub	autumn

Don't be fooled into thinking you can't grow fresh lemons in temperate climates, because you can. All it takes is basic know-how. Height 1.2m/4ft x 1.2m/4ft.

GROWING The hardiest and best variety for beginners is *Citrus limona* 'Meyer'. Plant the seedling in the minimum size pot since lemons dislike too big a container. Gradually plant up, using John Innes No 2 for young plants, incorporating John Innes No 3 once it reaches a 30cm/12in pot. Always ensure the soil has a plentiful supply of sharp sand for free-drainage. All repotting must be limited to spring and summer. From late autumn onwards restrict watering and in early spring prune and shape. At the same time commence giving a high nitrogen feed which improves foliage. Once the plant reaches the required height leave in the same pot and give an occasional root prune as necessary; also remove the top soil layer and add a top dressing. The fruit usually takes one year to ripen. Minimum temperatures of 10°C/50°F are required.

HARVESTING A good crop of small, tangy fruit in the autumn.

POSSIBLE PROBLEMS Don't be alarmed if the foliage goes yellow over winter. Mealy bug, scale insects.

■ COOK'S TIP

Make ice cream using this, or any soft fruit. Add 500 g / 1 lb of stoned apricots to a syrupy mix of sugar (50 g / 2 oz) and water (150 ml / ¼ pt). Heat for 12 minutes, *simmering gently. When cool add thick whipped cream to taste and then freeze overnight.*

■ COOK'S TIP

In Eliza Acton's 1861 cookery book she recommends filling a bottle with thin fresh lemon rinds and covering them with good brandy. Leave for *four weeks, strain off the spirit, and cork. Excellent when used as a flavouring, albeit one which is ruinously expensive.*

ORANGE

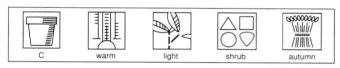

Three basic kinds are available – sweet oranges *(Citrus sinensis)*, bitter *(C. aurantium)*, and mandarin *(C. nobilis deliciosa)*. Within each group are a number of juicy varieties. The best choices for beginners are 'Malta Blood' (sweet), 'Chinotto' (bitter), and 'Satsuma' (mandarin). Height 1.2m/4ft x 1.2m/4ft.

GROWING Follow the same method as for lemon, buying and potting up a young shrub or grow from a pip. Sow just under a layer of John Innes No 1 in early spring and maintain at 21°C/70°F. Germination varies from a fortnight to one month. When the seedling is large enough to handle, move into a 7.5cm/3in pot and maintain at the same temperature. When the orange eventually develops into a young shrub prune in early spring if you want to restrict size. The plant will withstand a severe reduction every other year.

HARVESTING Although citrus plants are quite tough and can survive most frost-free temperatures, they need constant warmth (minimum 10°C/50°F) to produce fruit.

POSSIBLE PROBLEMS When mealy bugs or scale insects strike they leave behind a sticky substance which in turn attracts sooty mould. Spray to kill the insects and either wipe off the mould or, in severe cases, cut back the affected areas.

KIWI FRUIT

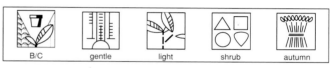

Also known as the Chinese gooseberry or *Actinidia chinensis*. It can easily reach 3m/10ft x 6m/20ft.

GROWING The small, furry covered, egg-size edible fruit appear on the female plant only, though a male is also required for pollination. Plant 3.6m/12ft apart. Thrives best in well-manured, fast-draining soil. Being hardy it can easily be grown outdoors but invariably it requires the extra warmth under glass for the fruit to ripen. In early spring in the first-year prune the shrub 30cm/12in above the soil. If allowed to grow unchecked it can grow enormous, therefore pinch out growing tips, and laterals at three leaves, when it has filled its allotted space. The fruit-bearing stems are kept to seven leaves beyond the last fruit. Initially prune in summer to produce more fruit; in following years prune over winter to thin tangled growth. Pollinate by hand.

HARVESTING After picking in early autumn store the fruit for 1 ½ months to let the flavour improve.

VARIETIES A. *arguta* is a 15m/50ft climber for outside walls, or growing up a tree, and has scented summer flowers. A. *kolomikta* is smaller at 3m/10ft. A. *polygama* scrambles up to 6m/20ft with unpleasant fruit. All have ornamental foliage.

POSSIBLE PROBLEMS Generally trouble-free.

■ COOK'S TIP

Oranges make a lively surprise salad with thinly sliced and whole radishes, green beans, and diced cucumber. Excellent with roast game.

■ COOK'S TIP

Make a refreshing summer sorbet by boiling 250 ml / 8 fl oz water with sparkling wine and sugar. Blend 1.75 kg / 3½ lb of puréed kiwi to the syrup and then leave to cool. Stir and sprinkle with finely grated lemon rind and finally freeze before serving with fresh fruit.

PINEAPPLE

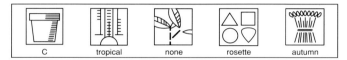

| C | tropical | none | rosette | autumn |

Fun to grow though note that only *Ananas comosus* is the true, edible pineapple. Other alternatives are *A. bracteatus* which has long, thin, sword-shaped leaves and blood red bracts. *A. b.* 'Striatus' has creamy variegated leaves. Height 90cm/36in x 1.5m/5ft.

GROWING *A. comosus* needs a minimum winter temperature of 18°C/65°F and good bottom heat if it is to fruit. Young plants should be potted on gradually until they are in 25-30cm/10-12in pots filled with two parts of fibrous loam, one part peat, one of sand. Plenty of water is required during the spring and summer, with a humid atmosphere. Keep the soil quite dry over winter. To propagate, slice away those suckers which appear around the base of the plant and pot up individually. Alternatively, remove the crown of an adult pineapple and pot up in a 10cm/4in pot of John Innes No 1 with a top layer of coarse sand. Cover with a polythene bag for added humidity and leave for two months at the above temperature. When the plant settles and puts on new growth remove the bag.

HARVESTING Pick the fruit when you can gently press your finger tips into the top, beneath the crown.

POSSIBLE PROBLEMS Generally trouble-free.

POMEGRANATE

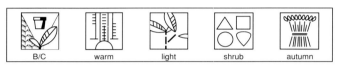

| B/C | warm | light | shrub | autumn |

The juicy pulp is a tasty, innovative addition for a fruit salad, and the juice makes a fine, iced drink. Height 2.4m/8ft x 2.4m/8ft.

GROWING Plant *Punica granatum* in a 30cm/12in pot filled with loam-, or peat-based compost, ideally John Innes No 2. Alternatively, sow seeds at 16°C/61°F, later transferring seedlings to 7.5cm/3in pots. For mature plants temperatures should be in the range of 7°C/45°F; any lower and the plant is unlikely to fruit. Watering at this period should be kept to a minimum. During spring and summer water freely giving a liquid feed every fortnight. In autumn, as the fruit develops, ensure the temperature is near 18°C/65°F. Pomegranate grown in a container must be potted up each spring to avoid becoming pot-bound. When the plant has reached the height you require you can root prune in the spring. In the wild, pomegranates grow as small trees 3m/10ft high.

HARVESTING Pick fruit when a burnt red colour, and slightly soft.

POSSIBLE PROBLEMS Generally trouble-free.

▨ COOK'S TIP

Make a pineapple fritter by mixing 125 g / 4 oz flour and a pinch of salt, and then add 1tbsp melted butter. Pour on 4 tbsp water, 150 ml / ¼ pt milk and one egg. Dip the sliced pineapple sections into the batter and deep fry. Particularly good with hot and spicy eastern food, or any chicken dish.

▨ GARDENER'S TIP

An attractive alternative to the fruiting pomegranate is the ornamental dwarf variety, P. granatum. It grows to 1.8m/6ft and flowers over summer.

PEACH/NECTARINE

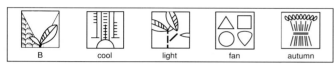

B	cool	light	fan	autumn

Though they are hardy enough to be grown outdoors, the best yield comes from plants grown under glass where there's guaranteed warmth. Use a lean-to against a sunny wall. Height 3m/10ft x 3m/10ft.

GROWING Plant over winter 30cm/12in away from the wall in extremely well drained, fertile soil. Lean the stem back so it can grow and be trained up a criss-cross of wires against the wall. Two weeks before planting add a scattering of general fertilizer. Thereafter add Growmore each spring. Train as a fan shape *(see page 105)*. More general pruning can only be carried out after late spring to avoid infection. For an early supply of fruit do not ventilate from early spring (unless temperatures exceed 15°C/60°F). Pollinate by hand, preferably at mid-day, and always maintain a moderately humid atmosphere by damping down. Thin the emerging fruitlets to three per cluster, and later to a distance of 15cm/6in.

HARVESTING Pick when plump and ripe. The fruit should easily come away if given a gentle, twisting tug.

POSSIBLE PROBLEMS Red spider mite. It helps to clean and whitewash the walls each (or every alternate) winter, untying the web of stems and easing them away from the wall.

STRAWBERRY

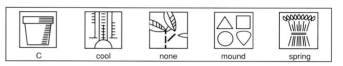

C	cool	none	mound	spring

Ideal for the cold greenhouse. The plants give an early supply of fruit and only take up greenhouse space from late winter to early spring.

GROWING Use new plants growing in 13cm/5in pots filled with John Innes No 2. Leave outdoors for the first part of winter, choosing a cold spot where the roots will get a good chilling. In mid-winter move them onto the greenhouse staging away from slugs and mice. As the plants start growing, begin watering and feeding with a general-purpose liquid feed. Beware of overwatering which rots the roots. Pollinate the flowers by hand in the absence of any insects and shade the emerging fruit from the fiercest sunlight. Good ventilation is essential on the hottest days. As the fruit significantly swell increase the amount of liquid feed. Plant out afterwards.

HARVESTING The best picking time varies according to variety. Flavour peaks with some fruit when the top half of the berry is red and the bottom tip cream coloured. Wait until the entire strawberry is bright red with others.

VARIETIES 'Cambridge Favourite'; 'Royal Sovereign'.

POSSIBLE PROBLEMS Avoid using the same forced plant two years running since fruit quality deteriorates.

▩ GARDENER'S TIP

Children enjoy growing peaches from seed. Plant a stone 5cm/2in deep in a pot of John Innes No 1 and leave on a windowsill. The cooler the room, the better. Water whenever the soil dries out and with luck a seedling should be visible after seven months. Grow until it's 30cm/12in high and then plant out.

▩ GARDENER'S TIP

For a fresh supply of strawberries pot-up 'runners' each summer. Each plant puts out a long stem, with new growth at the tip, which is planted in a 9cm/3½in pot of John Innes No 1. Cut the connecting stems when the young plant is well-rooted. Plant up to a 13cm/5in pot in early autumn.

VEGETABLES

Devoting an entire greenhouse to vegetables means you've more room to experiment with unusual varieties from specialist seed suppliers. Tall cucumbers, stem-tomatoes, French beans, sweet peppers, etc, can be spaced out so they don't flounder in each other's shadow. Good spacing also enables you to carry out a scrupulous 24-hour foliage examination to check against pest invasions.

HEAT Owners of cold greenhouses have two choices. Either wait for the end of the frosts before seed sowing, or provide the artificial heat of a propagator, timing the removal of the seedlings to coincide with decent temperatures. Don't be fooled by a splendid week in early spring because frosts can, and do, still strike. Outside, new growth is blasted, and under cover seedling tomatoes and courgettes react particularly badly. Growth is checked and can take weeks to recover. If you don't have a heated propagator, a house windowsill will suffice. Overcome the problem of one-directional light, and relatively poor growth, by lining

the sides of the seed tray with shiny foil. And with higher summer temperatures you don't need a heated propagator or greenhouse except for a few vegetables.

FRESH FERTILE SOIL Crop rotation is crucial under cover since pests and diseases quickly build up and proliferate in the extra warmth and humidity. Wireworms are another hazard. Sites previously laid to lawn are highly vulnerable and must be checked before sowing commences. By inserting three or four carrots into the ground and checking them every 24-hours you'll quickly discover if there's a problem. If there is take drastic action. Wet the soil with 600 ml/ 1 pt of 40 per cent commercial formaldehyde in 27 litres / 6 gallons of water, and cover the beds with sheeting for 24-hours so the fumes – lethal to all plants – take effect. When the sheets come off wait six weeks before planting. Throughout the treatment period ensure greenhouse doors, windows and flaps are kept open for maximum ventilation.

COLD FRAMES These are a good way of helping ease the problem of greenhouse overcrowding. Start off the hardier, container-grown vegetables inside and move them out in early summer. In between harden off the plants in cold frames, which are essentially holding areas where plants gradually acclimatize to their new environment. Cold frames can be bought for quick assembly but they are much cheaper to make yourself.

You need three wooden sides, higher at the back than the front so there's a forward sloping roof which lets in more light. Size obviously depends on your particular requirements but side panels at a height of 63.5cm/25in at the back and 30cm/12in at the front, and 75cm/30in wide should be fine. The back panel is a rectangle, 63.5cm/25in x 1.8m/6ft. And the front is 30cm/12in high x 1.8m/6ft. The roof is a wooden frame covered with polythene. French beans will not

French beans will not survive cold weather, so raise seedlings in the greenhouse or plant out in mid-spring and protect with a cold frame.

survive cold weather or savage frosts and should be raised as seedlings in the greenhouse, then moved outside when the temperature increases

Alternatively construct the cold frame around an old window pane. Initially keep it shut at night, but over the next week or so leave increasingly open – provided the weather is reasonable – by propping it up with bits of wood until the plant no longer needs protection against the elements. That way you clear the decks inside the greenhouse for another batch of crops.

MAJOR PESTS

Red spider mite It would be much more appropriated to refer to them as yellow-green mites since they aren't really red at all when active, though they do turn rust coloured in mid-autumn. To get a good look you may need a magnifying glass because they are minute, though that doesn't stop them causing mayhem. The mites pack the upper surfaces of young juicy leaves to suck the sap, leaving behind wrinkled, shrivelled vege-

tation, mottled leaves, and a silky web. They thrive in a dry atmosphere. Treat with insecticide sprayings in the evening when pollinating insects are absent. As a preventative measure, introduce the predatory mite *phytoseiulus persimilis* into the greenhouse.

Whitefly By far the commonest greenhouse nuisance. The moment you spot the tiny insect you must act, the problem invariably increases at an alarming rate and never disappears. Within 48-hours hundreds more insects will have spread to the underside of the juiciest leaves where they feed. A secondary problem is the honeydew deposits which lead to the spread of mould. Control both whitefly and blackfly by spraying with an insecticide in the evening. Alternatively the parasitic wasp *encarsia formosa* will devour the pest.

TOMATO PROBLEMS

Since tomatoes are prone to a wide range of problems, including whitefly, it's worth dealing with them in more detail.

Blossom rot The appearance of a dark crack at the top end of the fruit signifies calcium deficiency created by inadequate watering.

Blotchy patches Look out for bright yellow or dark green marks on the fruit which are caused by an absence of potash and/or nitrogen, roasting temperatures, and sunburn. Cure by increasing ventilation and watering.

Botyritis Created by poor ventilation and high humidity, and spreads both through wounded stems and on contact. As its name implies a grey fungus covers and rots plant tissue, though on tomato fruit you may instead see a watery green ring encircling a tiny spot. Botrytis also attacks lettuce and cucumbers.

Leafmould Appears doubly as a yellow blotch on the upper leaf and a bruise colour underneath. Cure by increasing ventilation to maintain a temperature of approximately 18°C/65°F and lower humidity levels.

Stem rot A fungal disease characterized by a speckled darkening of the stem created by spores which unless destroyed will attack the following summer. To be safe remove badly affected plants; more minor cases can be cured by cutting out the diseased areas.

Wilting The direct result of growing tomatoes in the same soil year after year. Only likely to occur in stale greenhouse beds.

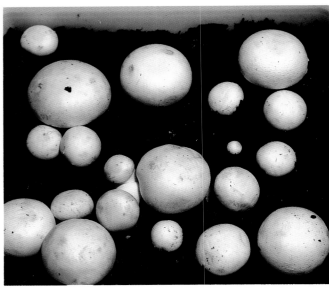

POTATO

| B/C | cool | 1.3cm/½in | 30cm/12in | 3 months |

Early varieties are easily raised. They're little trouble and provide first-rate flavour. If you don't have a border they can be grown in an old bucket with drainage holes, or even grow-bags.

GROWING Spread the seed in a tray in a cold, dark room in late winter and leave to sprout at a temperature of 5-7°C/40-45°F. Ensure the shoots are uppermost, and when they've reached 5cm/2in long plant in a container or bed. The free-draining soil should have been well-manured the previous autumn, with a handful of Growmore added two weeks before planting up. Avoid overwatering until the potato is putting out good foliage. Also avoid opening the greenhouse windows during frosty weather.

HARVESTING Young potatoes are ready for picking when the plant is 50cm/20in high. Thrust your hand into the soil and remove as many potatoes as you require. Once the weather outside improves, and the frosts are over, potatoes in containers and even grow-bags can be moved outside leaving room for new crops.

POSSIBLE PROBLEMS Watch out for aphids in early spring if there's been a particularly mild winter.

VARIETIES 'Pentland Javelin'; 'Ulster Chieftain'.

MUSHROOM

| C | tropical | 5cm/2in | 30cm/12in | 4 weeks |

A mushroom's natural habitat is in the damp, dark corner of a meadow, and these are precisely the conditions for which you've got to aim.

GROWING It's possible to make your own mushroom compost but far easier to buy ready made. The former requires decomposing straw (created by giving it a regular watering and forking over) subjected to a drying out period at 60°C/140°F. With a kit you simply mix the mushroom spawn with the compost and store at 18°C/65°F in a shady spot. At all times avoid direct sunlight. Two weeks later when threads of mycelium appear through the compost you add the special covering layer provided, which promotes mushroom devel- opment. With the re-appearance of the mycelium begin to water lightly, and slightly reduce the temperature by a couple of degrees. The first mushroom should appear as a pinhead within three weeks.

HARVESTING Occurs about one week after the first pin-heads have been sighted. The initial crop tends to be the largest, though you should get three to five more.

POSSIBLE PROBLEMS Avoid overwatering which results in mushroom rot, and excessive dryness.

▓ GARDENER'S TIP

Tempting though it is to accept a neighbour's supply of last year's tubers, always grow from fresh seed. The old supply will almost inevitably be infected with viruses. To store potatoes wrap them in old newspaper, never plastic bags, and leave on a garage shelf, in a cool, frost-free place.

▓ GARDENER'S TIP

If your garden consists of heavy clay soil then mushroom compost is an ideal way of helping break it up. Fork in large quantities over winter, with manure, and leafmould, even bags of horticultural grit. It has little nutritious value, but is an excellent soil conditioner.

SPAGHETTI MARROW

B	cool	3.5cm/1½in	1.5m/5ft	3 months

These marrows grow particularly well under glass. They get their name from the tasty spaghetti-like strands which are forked out and eaten after the squash has been boiled for 25 minutes. However do note that spaghetti marrows are rampant growers, and should only be raised in large greenhouses.

GROWING Use pre-germinated seeds and sow individually in pots in spring at a temperature of 18°C/65°F. Select the most vigorous seedling and plant in a quick-draining bed which has been well-manured the previous autumn. Alternatively, sow seeds in situ. It's advisable to keep three or four seedlings growing in reserve in case of problems. Once the marrow is under way they can be discarded. Raise like a courgette but provide plenty of cane and wire support against the greenhouse wall to contain the massive, sprawling growth. Regular watering is essential with added liquid feed. During incredibly hot dry spells put a layer of mulch over the soil.

HARVESTING Take regular pickings of young 20cm/8in fruit. The more frequently you pick, the more vigorously the marrow will put out new fruit.

POSSIBLE PROBLEMS Keep an eye out for aphids since they can be a major hazard. Inspect the marrow at least twice a day to guard against infestations.

SWEET CORN

B	warm	2.5cm/1in	45cm/18in	4 months

Always grow the plants by the greenhouse entrance and in blocks, so the wind can easily pollinate the flowers. If you can't do this you'll end up with a poor crop.

GROWING Getting the seeds to sprout can be tricky. The most reliable method involves laying them on wet tissue paper in a small box and covering with cling film. Place in a propagator at a temperature of 21°C/70°F until shoots appear, which should be within one week. Transfer four to each 7.5cm/3in peat pot to avoid subsequent root disturbance, and maintain at a minimum of 13°C/55°F. Thin to the strongest seedling and plant out in a well-manured bed. Provide a temperature of 13-18°C/55-65°F and only water liberally if the soil is in danger of drying out. Once the flowers emerge increase the rate of watering, with added liquid feed.

HARVESTING Most plants yield two cobs, sometimes one, but rarely three. Pick the moment they are ripe (when the paper-like covering has blackened). As a double check nick the cob to see whether it bleeds a thick whitish substance. Cook immediately and don't attempt to store because the sugar content quickly converts to starch and the taste is quite appalling.

POSSIBLE PROBLEMS Fruit fly larvae infect the stems.

▧ GARDENER'S TIP

Rest the developing fruit on slabs of wood, or bits of brick to keep them clear of the ground. Another possibility is sliced open plastic rubbish bags.

▧ COOK'S TIP

A highly unusual, brilliantly tasty dish is corn pancakes. Blanch the cob in milk, remove and then separate the corn. Mix together cream, egg and flour with the same milk, and add the segments of corn. Finally season to taste and cook in a large frying pan.

PEPPER

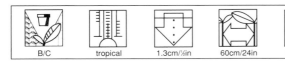

B/C	tropical	1.3cm/½in	60cm/24in	6/7months

Sweet peppers are not to be confused with small, hot chillies. They have a sweet flavour and add brilliant colour to salads.

GROWING You can grow sweet peppers in an unheated greenhouse, but you'll need to start them off in a propagator at temperatures of 21°C/70°F, and rely on summer-long temperatures of 18°C/65°F. Sow seeds in late winter, four per 9cm/3½in pot, and thin to the strongest seedling. In a heated greenhouse you can plant up to a 23cm/9in pot with John Innes No 3 in early spring, but otherwise wait until there's no more likelihood of frost. Alternatively, set out each plant in a bed 45cm/18in apart or three per grow bag. Since cold air checks fertilization keep the windows closed unless the temperature is 18°C/65°F. When the young fruits appear commence feeding at 14-day intervals with a liquid tomato feed, continuing until they turn red. By stopping the growing tips of a 15cm/6in high plant you increase bushiness. Stems must be tied to supporting canes.

HARVESTING Pick early for green fruit, late for a shiny red. Expect 8-20 peppers per plant.

POSSIBLE PROBLEMS Too dry a soil promotes shrivelled patches on the fruit.

VARIETIES F₁ hybrids 'Big Bertha', 'Gypsy'; 'New Ace'.

FRENCH BEAN

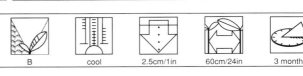

B	cool	2.5cm/1in	60cm/24in	3 months

You can grow either climbing beans tied to the full height of the greenhouse wall, or bushy dwarf varieties (45cm/18in high). The only difference between flageolet, kidney, haricot and green beans is that they are harvested at different times. Despite the name, the plant originates from South America.

GROWING A bright spot is essential. Fork manure into the well-dug bed, with additions of horticultural grit for fast drainage, over the preceding winter. Seeds for dwarf varieties are sown in early spring at 15°C/60°F in moist soil to encourage germination. In late spring the plant can be bedded-in and, to avoid weak, spindly growth prone to disease, provide excellent ventilation during warm weather. Plants growing in lightly manured soil will need an application of liquid feed whenever you water, but only provide when the soil becomes dry. Pampering the seedling before the flowers appear results in excessive amounts of leaf growth. Thereafter you can water more frequently.

HARVESTING Pick the pods when they are young and green, removing them gently to avoid damage.

POSSIBLE PROBLEMS Blackfly, greenfly; red spider mite frequently cluster beneath the leaves. Foot rot.

VARIETIES 'Hammond Dwarf Scarlet'; 'Gulliver'; 'Enorma'.

■ COOK'S TIP

Peppers are invaluable ingredients for a great cold ratatouille. Sauté onions, aubergines and the peppers in good quality olive oil. After 25 minutes add diced tomatoes, a sprinkling of coriander and garlic. After a further 10 minutes remove and serve cold. Dress with herbs.

■ PRESERVING TIP

The best way to make dry haricot beans is to leave all the pods on one plant, wait until the former have gone brown, and then dig up the plant. Store it in a cool, dry place and when the pods start to crack remove the beans. Keep in an airtight container, but note the longer you keep them the harder they get.

CUCUMBER

| B/C | tropical | 1.3cm/½in | 75cm/30in | 4 months |

Like courgettes they are highly productive. One plant can yield up to 25 cucumbers but they can be tricky in the early stages and need regular attention.

GROWING Sow seeds into a 9cm/3½in pot in spring when the temperature hits 21°C/70°F. Use peat-based John Innes No 1 and provide high humidity and a liquid feed. Before the plant becomes root-bound in early summer plant two per grow bag, or one in a 24cm/9⅞in pot filled with John Innes No 3. Beds must be well-manured beforehand, adding 50 per cent peat. Delay planting up during a cold spell or growth will suffer. Provide plant support using 1.8m/6ft canes, or taut string wedged under the plant and secured to the greenhouse roof. Tying-in also avoids a huge tangled mess of tendrils. Remove all the male flowers (the female's have a swelling under the bloom) to avoid bitter fruit. Cucumbers grow on side branches – only allow one per axil and stop it once the fruit forms (ie after two leaves). If you don't keep it under control the plant will quickly become exhausted.

HARVESTING It is beneficial to pick frequently at a reasonable size (30cm/12in) since flavour diminishes when the fruit gets too big.

POSSIBLE PROBLEMS Chiefly red spider mite and whitefly.

COURGETTE

| B | cool | 4cm/1¾in | 90cm/36in | 3 months |

Courgettes and marrows are one and the same, the only difference being size. When the young fruit is approximately 20cm/8in long it is a sweet-tasting courgette. Marrows can easily grow to 30cm/12in.

GROWING Sow seeds individually in peat pots in spring, either in a heated propagator or when the greenhouse temperature hits 18°C/65°F. After six weeks the plant should have four leaves and be ready for bedding in. Plants in beds with minimum supplies of manure should be given a liquid feed once a fortnight. The male and female flowers (the former is flat behind the flower, the latter has a noticeable swelling) open regularly throughout the summer, but when this coincides with a cold spell you must pollinate artificially. Pick the male and insert into a maximum of three females.

HARVESTING Pick regularly and often over summer.

POSSIBLE PROBLEMS Overwatering and/or poor drainage yields withered fruit. In extreme cases bad drainage leads to foot rot in which case the plant must be destroyed.

VARIETIES Round courgettes (eg 'Rondo de Nice') are particularly succulent; 'Zucchini' (green); 'Gold Rush', 'Eldorado' (yellow).

■ COOK'S TIP

For a cucumber salad with a bit of zing slice into 5cm/2in strips, and add to a mixture of thinly diced onion with parsley. Sprinkle on vinegar *(preferably fruit flavoured) and olive oil. Add seasoning and finally sweeten to taste with sugar.*

■ COOK'S TIP

For a surprise side-dish quickly boil the yellow courgette flowers and then drain. Next stuff their trumpets with oil-fried diced courgette and *tomatoes, season with basil, salt and pepper. Allow to cool before stuffing. Handle gently at all stages.*

LETTUCE

| B/C | cool | 1.3cm/½in | 30cm/12in | 2/3 months |

Best grown as early spring or late autumn crops to supplement the wider range of easily grown, outdoor summer varieties.

GROWING Provide a minimum temperature of 7°C/45°F, and sow half-a-dozen seeds into a number of peat pots filled with John Innes No 1. When the seedlings emerge, thin to one vigorous shoot per pot, and plant in a bed or large container with drainage holes. Avoid transplanting thereafter since they dislike root disturbance and tend to bolt or suffer checked growth. During cold spells pack straw round the plants to maintain warmth. Initially water in well, always in the morning, but afterwards avoid overdoing it unless the weather is unusually hot and dry.

HARVESTING Once a small heart is visible the lettuce is ready for cutting. Don't expect particularly large centres with out-of-season crops because they don't produce them. Slice off the lettuce and throw the stem section onto the compost heap.

POSSIBLE PROBLEMS Overwatering leads to an attack of mildew.

VARIETIES 'Little Gem' for an early sowing; 'Kwiek', and 'Marmer' for late summer sowing.

RADISH

| B/C | cool | 6mm/¼in | 10cm/4in | 2 months |

A packet of salad radish seed is excellent for sowing between main crops in the greenhouse border. They take up little room, and add extra bite and flavour to hot and cold dishes.

GROWING From late winter on sow seeds in a frost-free greenhouse, ideally at 7°C/45°F, in small, well-raked drills. Scatter on Growmore two weeks before sowing. Note that excessive watering leads to an abundance of leaf, and too little creates bolting and woody, spongy, inedible radishes. As the seedlings appear, thin out. If left too tightly packed together they force each other out of the ground. As an alternative to summer radishes try the winter variety which has a white, carrot-like growth. Sow in summer, and harvest in mid-autumn for eating with a winter roast, cooking the radishes like turnips.

HARVESTING Approximately two months after an early sowing you should have a row of fat, bright red radishes. Pick and eat. Summer sowings will be ready in half the time. To guarantee a regular supply, sow a handful of seed every two weeks.

POSSIBLE PROBLEMS Pick the moment the radishes are ready. If left in the ground for too long they quickly deteriorate. Also beware of club root.

▩ COOK'S TIP

Try experimenting with Chinese stem lettuce. It tastes more like a nutty cucumber and can be used raw or cooked. The stems are peeled and the underlying flesh either goes straight onto a salad or is stir-fried. The Chinese also use it in soups. The young leaves are best boiled like greens.

▩ COOK'S TIP

Sliced radishes make a brightly coloured top layer for salads. By buying packets of different coloured radishes, and growing a few of each at every sowing, you dramatically heighten the effect. Colours include red and white, pinkish-red, crimson and scarlet, in round and finger-like shapes.

TOMATO

| B/C | cool | 5mm/⅛in | 56cm/22in | 6 months |

Since tomatoes have an intense dislike of the cold they provide far better quality fruit under glass. But in the greenhouse they're pretty demanding and require constant pampering. Bush tomatoes require less effort, but they flop all over the place and are really for outdoors.

GROWING Either sow early spring in a heated propagator providing seeds with a temperature of 18°C/65°F, or wait until there's a hot week in early spring. Germination takes less than a fortnight under a fine covering of vermiculite. When the seedlings develop, thin to the strongest and plant up to a 7.5cm/3in pot. Leave until the first flowers appear (when the plant is some 20cm/8in tall) and then transfer to a grow-bag, bed, or 23cm/9in pot filled with John Innes No 3. Water sparingly to avoid plant wilt, and add a liquid tomato feed. As the fruit appear, so both can be increased. Snap off side shoots growing in the leaf axils, and when the fourth truss of fruit has set, stop the main growing point. Grow up a cane or a taut piece of string wedged under the plant's root system at one end, and tied to the greenhouse roof at the other.

HARVESTING By mid-summer when the plant is 1.5m/5ft tall the first crop will be ripening.

POSSIBLE PROBLEMS see page 113.

AUBERGINE

| B/C | tropical | 1cm/½in | 60cm/24in | 5 months |

Otherwise known as 'egg-plants', aubergines come in two colours, purple and white. The purple are excellent for Mediterranean type dishes, and the white for pickling.

GROWING Raise as an annual, sowing the particularly slow-growing seeds in spring at 21°C/70°F using John Innes No 1. Transfer the seedlings to 9cm/3½in pots when they're large enough to handle, and reduce the heat to 18°C/65°F. After three months proceed to plant up individually into 30-38cm/12-15in pots with John Innes No 2, or two plants per grow-bag. Alternatively, use the greenhouse border. Feed with a liquid tomato fertilizer and never allow the plant to dry out. The best policy is 'little and often'. Growing the plant up string or canes is not essential, though for the sake of tidiness the latter is useful, in which case three 1.2m/4ft lengths are ideal for tying-in. For a bushier specimen stop the growing tip when the plant is 15cm/6in high, and only allow six fruit per plant.

HARVESTING The fruit will be ready for picking from early autumn. Either pick the young aubergines regularly when they are just big enough to use, or allow a maximum of six decent size fruits per plant.

POSSIBLE PROBLEMS Look out for aphids, whitefly and particularly red spider mite.

◼ GARDENER'S TIP

If you're going to be away a lot and can't get a neighbour to tend the tomatoes try ring culture. Grow the plants in a bottomless pot which stands on a bed of pebbles and stones. The roots work down into this layer and are far less prone to drying out.

◼ GARDENER'S TIP

If the aubergine tastes bitter, thinly slice the fruit on a large plate, spread out, sprinkle over with salt and lemon juice and leave to stand for about ½ an hour.

HERBS

The following line-up of herbs divides into three categories. The uncomplicated (parsley), the mildly exotic (basil from Mexico and Thailand, etc), and the totally exotic (ginger) only for those with high-performance, super-sophisticated greenhouses. Whichever category you prefer note there are scores more herbs to tackle. For the best range hunt out a herb seed specialist because they are constantly tracking down excellent new varieties from abroad which garden centres rarely stock.

POTS Check which part of the world the seeds come from and reproduce their natural growing conditions. For instance garden thyme *(Thymus vulgaris)* comes from the Mediterranean where it grows on warm, sunny hillsides. The landscape is not covered in John Innes No 2 but uncompromising stoney ground where goats not people predominate. In summer the landscape is scorching, drenched by the occasional, massive downpour. So if you've got a wretched, cold wet

summer try and put your thyme under glass. Two bad summers like that and the plant will amount to nothing. Otherwise don't pamper it and put a thick layer of drainage material at the bottom of the pot for the roots to snake through.

HERB GARDEN The second reason for growing herbs under glass is that protected from severe spring frosts, they'll provide an early summer crop. Later, most will benefit hugely from a spell outside. Since there's going to be plenty of ferrying plants between the herb garden and the greenhouse, try and juxtapose the two areas. Also divide up the herb garden for easy access to the pots to be brought back indoors over winter. A simple, neat design is a circle divided into six triangular segments. Paths run between each, and right round the perimeter.

If you feel the centre of the herb circle needs a special feature try a stone plinth, or alternatively an old stone trough for herbs. Since it's virtually impossible to find these troughs anymore, let alone at a reasonable price, you could always make yours from a kitchen sink.

STONE SINKS To convert one into the other, use the following recipe.

1 Scrub down a kitchen sink in the greenhouse. Take off the taps and unblock the plug hole of any accumulated debris.

2 Mix a special paste. This consists of one part cement, one of peat, and two of sand. Add water to create an oozy sticky substance which you spread across the outside surface of the sink, and just over the rim of the top onto the inside. Smooth with a piece of wood and leave to set for 48-hours.

3 Finish off with the paint – in this case milk mixed with cow manure. It gives a natural-looking, dark green colour.

4 Fill the interior with pots, or stones and pebbles for quick drainage and then heap in the soil with sharp sand. The sink can now be permanently planted up.

PRESERVING One of the key attractions of growing herbs is that you can preserve the leaves and the scent. The most effective drying programme involves speed, darkness, good air circulation and heat. The temperature range must lie within 21°C/70°F and 29°C/85°F and is best provided by an oven or an airing cupboard with the door left open. The best method is to scatter the leaves on a piece of muslin lining a tray, and wait until they are crackly and stiff. The leaves should be green at the end of the drying period and definitely not black - a clear sign of excessive heat. The time taken depends upon the quantity of leaves, oven size, leaf moisture content, and the degree of air circulation. Afterwards store immediately in airtight glass jars in a dark room.

An alternative is to freeze the herbs. This is simpler though not necessarily such a reliable method. It involves cutting the stems early in the morning when the volatile oils are at their strongest, washing and shaking off as much moisture as possible, and finally inserting the leaves in airtight plastic bags. They are now ready to freeze.

In the foreground of this four part, easily accessible, herb border is yellow marjoram surrounded by calendula making a delightful display, as well as satisfying the culinary palate.

TOPIARY Young rosemary plants are the best choice: they should be approximately 7.5cm/3in high, and their stems still supple. The choice of shape is entirely up to you; abstract geometry or classical.

To create a vertical spiral, for example, insert three 1.2m/4ft canes in a triangle in the pot. Next, take a length of stiff wire and attach one end to the base of one cane. Proceed to wrap it upwards and around all three canes. Take time getting it symmetrical because this will be the shape of the rosemary and mistakes can't be rectified years later. Finally, plant the well-rooted rosemary cutting in the centre and loosely tie the tip to the wire, gradually training it up the spiral.

Keep removing side branches so the plant's energy is chanelled into extending the growing tip. It's worth growing two spiral shapes in case a) of an accident in which case you have one in reserve, b) it turns out better than expected so you can pair them off to either side of a door, and c) you've got a ready made present. Keep under glass for maximum growing conditions.

121

CORIANDER

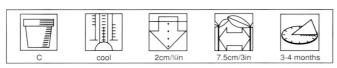

| C | cool | 2cm/¾in | 7.5cm/3in | 3-4 months |

Two kinds are available, Moroccan *Coriandrum sativum* (*above*) which is traditionally used for a good crop of aromatic seeds. And Cilantro *C. s.* which produces larger quantities of feathery leaves which are invaluable in eastern cuisine, being used rather like parsley. The flavour is much sharper and rather lemony.

GROWING Use a wide shallow terracotta pot, or alternatively a plastic mushroom box with drainage holes pierced through the bottom. In spring fill with multipurpose compost, sow, cover lightly and water. Thereafter water seedlings as required and then place the container in the sunniest position. The leaves are at their most aromatic just before the small white flowers open. The small round beige seedheads can be gathered in the autumn and either stored whole in an airtight container or ground down to a fine powder. The sooner it is used the better. After several months it begins to smell like cardboard.

POSSIBLE PROBLEMS Generally trouble-free.

USES Add to meat or chicken curries for flavour and the bright green leaf colour.

MINT

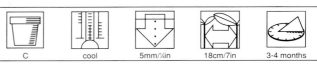

| C | cool | 5mm/¼in | 18cm/7in | 3-4 months |

An ornamental pot with three or four different kinds of mint makes a fine present. Keep in the greenhouse over winter, away from the fiercest frosts, for an early spring crop of varied flavours.

GROWING Raise either from seed or by division. Fill a 23cm/9in pot with multipurpose compost and divide the surface area into three or four sections, planting a different kind of mint in each – say apple, pineapple, ginger and spearmint. Ensure their final heights will be roughly equal or one kind will swamp the others. Cover the seeds with a thick layer of soil and water. When the seedlings appear, thin to the strongest of each variety. When each stem is 5cm/2in tall pinch back to encourage bushiness. Over summer, leave outside in dappled sunlight/shade so the soil isn't continuously drying out. In late autumn bring under glass.

HARVESTING Use for culinary purposes just before flowering when the scent is at its strongest.

POSSIBLE PROBLEMS Since mint is an invasive plant don't expect the three/four neat divisions in the pot to last long. Not that that matters. Part of the fun is in identifying the different flavours.

USES In iced cold drinks as well as on salads and cooked vegetables, potatoes etc.

▇ PRESERVING TIP

Keep fresh by picking the coriander with roots, and placing it in water. Put inside a polythene bag and then refrigerate for several weeks.

▇ COOK'S TIP

Mix butter, diced mint leaves, seasoning (salt and pepper) with lemon juice. Work to a creamy texture, roll into golf-size balls and refrigerate until needed.

GARLIC

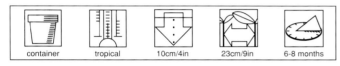

| container | tropical | 10cm/4in | 23cm/9in | 6-8 months |

Essential for anyone who cares about food. Pluck your own bulbs fresh and zingy from the soil.

GROWING For a handful of large succulent garlic, plant outside in pots over winter and bring indoors the following summer. First, buy the largest, healthiest garlics available and detach the bulbs. Plant out (point uppermost) in mid-autumn, 10cm/4in deep in free draining sandy loam in a large plastic container. Bury the latter in the ground so it's level with the surrounding soil. Garlic is extremely hardy and will tolerate temperatures of -10°C/14°F. The following spring remove the containers from the ground and leave outside for a fortnight. Acclimatize them to temperatures inside the greenhouse and eventually leave in permanent warmth. The bulbs put on maximum growth at around 20°C/68°F in early summer.

HARVESTING When the onion-like green leaves turn brown and start to die down, lift and use. Handle with care since they easily bruise.

POSSIBLE PROBLEMS Heavy wet clay soils are highly unsuitable.

USES Roasted individually; in stews and curries; pasta sauces.

BORAGE

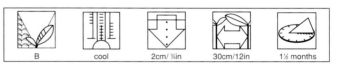

| B | cool | 2cm/¾in | 30cm/12in | 1½ months |

A sturdy annual good for its blue, star-shaped flowers and cucumber tasting leaves.

GROWING In mid-spring sow seeds of this 60cm/24in high herb in the greenhouse border. The drills should be approximately 30cm/12in apart, consisting of light, free-draining soil in full sun. The plant flowers until the first bad frost, though it can easily last to Christmas in a mild spell. Beware its tendency to self-seed which is fine outdoors but can be a potential greenhouse nightmare. Pluck out seedlings that root where they are not wanted or you could end up with an invasion. When sown in early spring, given mild weather, borage flowers in the greenhouse after two and then four months, seeding to give a third display in late summer.

POSSIBLE PROBLEMS Generally trouble-free.

USES Since borage has a rather salty taste it is an invaluable ingredient for those cutting down on their salt intake. Also, try the leaves in a glass of Pimms, a fruit cocktail, or cheap and cheerful red wine. When drying borage leaves use only the youngest, and keep the oven at a low temperature. If dried quickly they should retain their distinctive aroma stored in an airtight container.

▓ PRESERVING TIP

Garlic will keep for six months. Either braid the stems and hang, or lay flat, in a cool, dry, airy room. When brown spots appear it is no longer useable.

▓ ORGANIC TIP

Borage is known as beebread because its scent and star-like blue flowers attract bees. Plant by the door of the greenhouse for pollinating.

123

BASIL

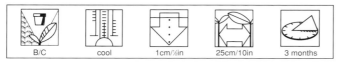

B/C	cool	1cm/½in	25cm/10in	3 months

An annual herb excellent for salads and making home-made pesto. A good seed specialist should have a minimum of 12 varieties, ranging from Greek to Indonesian.

GROWING In late spring after the last of the frosts, fill however many mini pots you require with seed compost and scatter four seeds onto each. Give a light covering of soil, and water. Either place in a heated propagator at 13°C/55°F, or wait for the cold greenhouse temperature to rise. When the seedlings appear, thin to the strongest in each pot. Water gently to begin with, and thereafter whenever the soil dries out. It's better to wait for the leaves to wilt slightly and let the plant tell you when it needs a drink than to overwater. When the plant becomes root-bound pot up to the next size and add John Innes No 1; at the last potting up use No 2. Commence giving a liquid feed every 10 days. Pinch out the growing tips for a bushy specimen and never let the plant flower or it promptly loses its flavour.

HARVESTING Pick dark green, shiny leaves.

POSSIBLE PROBLEMS On a very hot day ensure they don't keel over for lack of water.

USES Whole basil leaves scattered on sliced red peppers and covered with garlic/olive oil taste delicious.

PARSLEY

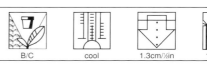

B/C	cool	1.3cm/½in	15cm/6in	4/5 months

Three basic kinds are available: the traditional, curly leaf *(above)*; fern-leaf; and giant Italian parsley. Cooks should use the latter since it's got the strongest flavour.

GROWING The seed takes a long time to germinate – up to five weeks – and needs constant warmth. Either raise in a heated propagator at around 21°C/70°F, or wait until the weather strikes a warm spell in spring. Fill pots with seed compost or, if you are sowing large quantities, half-fill plastic boxes with garden soil and add a top layer of seed compost. Scatter on the seeds, cover and water regularly. When the seedlings appear, thin to distances of 7.5cm/3in and later to 20cm/8in. The reject seedlings can be used for cooking. Feed the mature plants with a liquid fertilizer and place in the shadiest spot. Parsley is frost-tolerant and will survive in an unheated greenhouse over winter while temperatures outside dive to -10°C/14°F. Keep until next year's crop appears and then discard.

HARVESTING Nip out selectively to encourage bushiness.

POSSIBLE PROBLEMS Bolting (caused by under-watering in hot spells).

USES Besides its excellent flavour it has strong colour and a high vitamin content.

◼ COOK'S TIP

To make pesto, mix ground basil leaves with salt, garlic and pine nuts. Add parmesan or sardo cheese, and finally pour on olive oil. Mix until the paste is smooth. If storing omit the garlic; add at the time of use since it doesn't keep and goes rancid.

◼ PRESENTATION TIP

Grow in a special parsley terracotta pot, which has openings not just at the top but also right round the container. Makes a marvellous gift.

TARRAGON

C	warm	1.3cm/½in	90cm/36in	4 months

The choice is between the French variety *(Artemisia dracunculus)* and the Russian *(A. dracunculoides)*. The French has a real tangy flavour but isn't too hardy and will not survive a bad frost so greenhouse-growing is essential. Cooks should not compromise – Russian tarragon has zero taste.

GROWING Poor, stony, free-draining soil in a hot spot is essential, being similar to its natural Mediterranean habitat. If growing in a container use a large pot because tarragon is a vigorous grower, and limit yourself to three plants per 23cm/9in container. Avoid feeding because the plant becomes too succulent and is unlikely to survive the winter. Propagate by division in spring or autumn.

HARVESTING Pick regularly to encourage new growth.

POSSIBLE PROBLEMS Eliminate the likelihood of disease and loss of vigour by dividing every four years and planting up the youngest growth.

USES Make a strong spiky tarragon sauce by splashing wine vinegar over scraps of bread, adding tarragon and garlic, and finally olive oil. Quickly blend and season.

GINGER

C	tropical	20cm/8in	25cm/10in	11 months

Ginger is now such an essential part of everyday cuisine it's sensible to grow your own provided you can guarantee the right conditions. Note, they are pretty demanding.

GROWING Select a rhizome with a good array of buds. Plant in a pot packed with plenty of rich, well-manured soil in spring. Water and mulch over for approximately three weeks to give added warmth and help it into growth. In the meantime provide a temperature of approximately 21°C/70°F and regularly spray the greenhouse floor to maintain high humidity. A small number of shoots can be cut and eaten when they are 10cm/4in high, being regarded as a splendid delicacy. Japanese ginger is grown for its flowers which are picked pre-flowering and used in recipes. This rhizome is inedible.

HARVESTING After nearly one year the rhizome can be lifted, stored, and used in recipes.

POSSIBLE PROBLEMS Generally trouble-free.

USES Ginger biscuits and bread; puddings; home-made ginger beer. It can be sliced, grated, chopped, or used as a paste with water and garlic.

▓ DRYING TIP

Remove stems when the flowers appear and dry in an oven at around 32°C/90°F, certainly not much higher. Handle with care since the leaves easily bruise which adversely affects the volatile oils. Store in an airtight container in a dark room.

▓ COOK'S TIP

A traditional Arab drink served at the birth of a baby goes as follows. Boil 1 litre /1 ¾ pts of water for 5 minutes with ground ginger, aniseed (1 tbsp), two cloves and a cinnamon stick. Sweeten according to taste. It might sound uninviting but is quite delicious and invigorating.

GLOSSARY

Acid Used to describe soil with a pH of below 7.0.
Since acid soils contain little lime, extra lime must be added

Alkaline A soil with a pH reading above 7.0.
A slightly alkaline soil suits most plants

Annual A plant that completes its life cycle in one growing season

Axil The angle between the leaf and the stem, from which new growth emerges

Bedding plant A plant used for temporary garden display

Biennial A plant requiring two seasons to complete its life cycle

Bolt Running to seed prematurely

Bonemeal A phosphatic fertilizer also containing small amounts of nitrogen

Bract A modified leaf which may be coloured and have the appearance of a petal

Bromeliad Any of a family of tropical American plants, typically epiphytes with a rosette of fleshy leaves

Calyx Sepals of a flower that collectively protect the developing flower

Cloche Glass or plastic covering to protect plants in the open

Compost A mixture of loam, sand, peat and leaf-mould used for growing plants in containers. Also, the rotted remains of plant and other organic material

Corm A plant storage organ. At the top is the bud from which new shoots and new roots appear

Corolla The inner leafy whorl of a flower's petals

Crocks Broken pieces of clay pots

Crown The bottom of a perennial from which roots and shoots arise

Damping down Watering the greenhouse in warm weather to increase humidity

Deadhead Removing faded flowerheads to prevent seeding and encourage further flowering. Also to keep the plant looking tidy

Dormant The period when a plant is resting, usually winter

Drill Narrow grove made in soil in order to receive seeds which are consequently sown in straight lines

Epiphyte A plant that grows on another plant but is not a parasite on it

Ericaceous Lime-free compost

Evergreen A plant which bears foliage throughout the year (and sometimes no flowers)

F_1 (first generation) A seed strain obtained by two pure-bred, closely related varieties

Fertilization The fusion of male and female plant elements (ie pollen and undeveloped seed) to form a mature seed

Force Hurrying plants into growth by use of heat or some other means. Bulbs may be forced by putting the pots outside in a cool place for two months, before bringing them into the greenhouse

Fungicide A substance used to combat fungal disease

Germination The first stage in the development of a plant from seed

Half-hardy A plant which requires protection over winter

Hardening off Acclimatizing plants from a sheltered environment to outside conditions

Hardy Plants which can survive frost

Heel A cutting with a piece of the old wood attached

Humus The substance remaining when dead vegetable matter has broken down

Insecticide A substance used to kill insects

Lateral A stem or shoot that emerges from the leaf axil of a larger stem

Leader The main stem of a shrub/tree that extends the system of branches

Larva The immature stage of some insects, eg caterpillars and grubs

Loam Soil which is a compound of clay, silt, sand and humus. It is moisture-retentive and mineral rich

Mulch A layer of organic material spread on the soil surface to conserve moisture

Neutral A soil with a pH reading between 6.5 and 7.0, being neither acid nor alkaline

Offset A young plant naturally produced by mature plants and which can be detached and used for propagation

Organic Substances which are the product of decaying, living organisms

Peat Partially decayed organic matter. Sedge peat comes from the roots of edges growing in bogs

Perennial A plant that lives for an indefinite period

pH reading The pH scale denotes the level of acidity or alkalinity in the soil. A neutral reading is 7.0; above that denotes alkalinity, below acidity

Pinching out Removing the growing point of a stem to encourage bushy growth

Pitcher Plant Any of various insectivorous plants. The leaves are modified to form pitcher-like organs that attract and trap insects, which are then digested

Pollination Transferring pollen grains from the male to female flowers

Pricking out Planting out seedlings

Propagation Increasing plants

Pruning Cutting back a plant to keep the shape neat, restrict size, and encourage flower formation

Root run The soil area occupied by a plant's roots

Runner An aerial stem which roots at the tip when it touches soil

Seedling A young plant

Self-fertile A fruit tree which does not require pollinators to set fruit

Spadix A spike of flowers of a fleshy stem

Spathe A large bract that encloses the inflorescence of several members of the lily family

Sucker A shoot that arises from below soil level

Tender Any plant susceptible to frost damage

Transplant Moving young plants from place to place, so giving them more room to develop

Vine Eyes

INDEX